MINOR PROPHETS
by Nancy Fink

2018 One Stone Press.
All rights reserved. No part of this book may be reproduced
in any form without written permission of the publisher.

Published by:
One Stone Press
979 Lovers Lane
Bowling Green, KY 42103

Printed in the United States of America

ISBN 13: 978-1-941422-24-3

Supplemental Materials Available:

~ Answer Key

~ Downloadable PDF

www.onestone.com

We want to thank Manna Bible Maps for allowing the use of their maps on Paul's Journeys. These maps and others can be purchased and downloaded from www.biblemaps.com.

1.800.428.0121
www.onestone.com

CONTENTS

	Timeline of the Minor Prophets	7
Lesson 1	The Minor Prophets	9
Lesson 2	Hosea	15
Lesson 3	Joel	23
Lesson 4	Amos	29
Lesson 5	Obadiah	37
Lesson 6	Jonah	43
Lesson 7	Micah	49
Lesson 8	Nahum	55
Lesson 9	Habakkuk	61
Lesson 10	Zephaniah	67
Lesson 11	Haggai	73
Lesson 12	Zechariah	79
Lesson 13	Malachi	87

Acknowledgements

Great appreciation and heartfelt thanks goes to Amy Bruns and Donna Jo Nash who are scholarly Bible students, teachers and historians. Their knowledge of biblical and world history has been invaluable to the making of this project. These two godly women have helped me stay on task and have edited this work for accuracy to the Scriptures.

Special thanks goes to Nya Taylor. Nya was the patient fifth grade reader who carefully read the manuscripts to make sure she understood what I was trying to say about these colorful prophets. I am thankful for her participation and red marker pen!

Lastly, my thanks goes to my loving, supportive husband who also helped balance my sentences, made suggestions, and listened patiently as I droned on for hours about the exciting stories revealed in the 12 short books known as simply, The Minor Prophets. I hope the readers of this book will get excited about these ancient, bold and dedicated messengers of God and will want to dig deeper into God's Holy Book for more treasures.

Dedication

This book is dedicated to my young friend, student, and brother in the Lord, Nicholas "Nikki" Negron. It was my distinct privilege to work with Nikki in the Roswell Bible Lab and watch him learn, grow and develop in his knowledge, love and appreciation for God and His word. Watching Nikki's faith blossom was a wonderful thing, even more amazing was watching his love and total trust in God spread to all who were fortunate enough to know him. Nikki was a truly amazing young man who drew strength from God's Holy Word. Nikki's complete confidence in the Lord's ability to deliver on His promises will continue to glow in my heart until the Lord calls me home. It is my sincere desire that this meager effort to relate the treasures found in the Minor Prophets will help young Bible students to close their knowledge "gap."

Forward

Sundays have always been my favorite day of the week. Not only is it a fresh start to a new week but, as a youth, I couldn't wait to get to Bible class to be with my friends and hear another awesome story about God's people who lived so long ago. In Sunday school classes, I heard all those wonderful Old Testament stories about Creation, Noah and the ark, Abraham, Joseph bringing his family into Egypt and then after 400 years, Moses leading the now huge family of Israel, out of Egypt. (Wow, talk about over staying your welcome!) We learned about Joshua leading God's people into the Promised Land, and how Israel became a strong nation under Kings Saul, David and Solomon. I always thought it interesting that God not only recorded the good things these Bible heroes accomplished but also the bad things. The not-so-good details made me realize that even God's people really mess up at times. Our God is so great! When they stopped doing the things that made Him angry, prayed for His forgiveness, and turned again to obey Him, He forgave and forgot the bad things they had done.

After King Solomon's death, the kingdom divided. The 10 northern tribes become known as Israel and the 2 southern tribes as Judah. Right around the time of the divided kingdom, the fog begins to creep into my memory as to what comes next. Even though we are only two-thirds of the way through the Old Testament, the stories and characters are jumbled into disjointed events. I had no idea historically how the remainder of the Bible stories and characters fit or their relevance to the theme of the Bible. Happily, sprinkled into the mixture of Sunday school fog are the great stories of Elijah and the 'showdown' at Mount Carmel with the false prophets of Baal. I even recall Elisha calling a 'she bear' to maul some mean boys for calling him "baldy" and if I remember correctly, Elisha did have a bald head. Every one remembers the story of Daniel in the lions' den although probably could not tell you where it fits into God's big picture of the Bible, and then...and then...well, now we come to the problem. For some reason all those great Old Testament stories with their colorful characters come to a sudden stop. Students find themselves leaping over a giant gap of several hundred years right into the New Testament to be introduced to the births of John the Baptist and baby Jesus.

So, what happened? How did we get from Old Testament into the New Testament so quickly? What's in the gap? What is the deal with those 12 little books, the Minor Prophets, located behind the lengthy books known as Major Prophets? Other than a quick lesson about Jonah and the big fish, I couldn't tell you what those 12 little books are about or even why the Holy Spirit bothered to have them written and placed in the Bible.

Sadly, there are many who have experienced the same 'gap' in their Bible knowledge. These 12 little books of the Minor Prophets are packed with information, warnings and hope. They show us how God dealt with His people of long ago and give us a clear picture of how He is going to deal with us today if we behave like those rebellious people of old.

Reading the Minor Prophets gives us a better understanding of God, His love, patience, and desire for mankind to have a loving and strong relationship with Him. What we learn is that when man chooses his own way and not God's way, there are consequences **every** time. They show the severity of God's anger and teach man that God does not give man a 'time-out session,' or put him on restriction for being stubborn and hardheaded. The consequences for ignoring God have devastating and eternal consequences.

The first time I started to love and appreciate the 12 colorful books of the Minor Prophets, was when I took the time to look at a Bible timeline and saw just when in history these prophets worked. I found out what was going on during their time of history and to whom they were sent to warn. It became even more of a passion when I realized how Christians today should see the mistakes of the people of old and realize that God does not change (Malachi 3:6). He **always** keeps His promises. It would be wise for all of us to pay attention to the warnings of the Minor Prophets and realize that this is how God deals with rebellious, stubborn, and prideful people, even the people of today.

The Minor Prophets are packed full of references to the coming of Jesus, the Messiah. These books should give hope and comfort to God's faithful. They teach us that even though man's sins require punishment, God cares for His faithful, even during the hard times of judgment. God loves us so much that He sent His only Son, the perfect sacrifice, to die as payment for our sins (John 3:16).

It is my hope to help students understand the treasures that are found in the 12 little books called the Minor Prophets. They are only referred to as 'minor' because of the length of their writings in comparison to that of the Major Prophets.' Their writings demonstrate God's love for all mankind. He is a just God and will punish the unrighteous. There doesn't need to be a 'gap' in our appreciation of who God is and how He deals with nations. These 12 short books are vital to understanding the Big Picture of the Bible story. Come explore and be ready to unlock the giant messages from God contained in these tiny but powerful books of the Minor Prophets.

> *"In the past God spoke to our ancestors through the prophets. He spoke to them many times and in many different ways. And now in these last days God has spoken to us through his Son..."*
> Hebrews 1:1-2 (ICB)

Timeline of the Minor Prophets ▶ 7

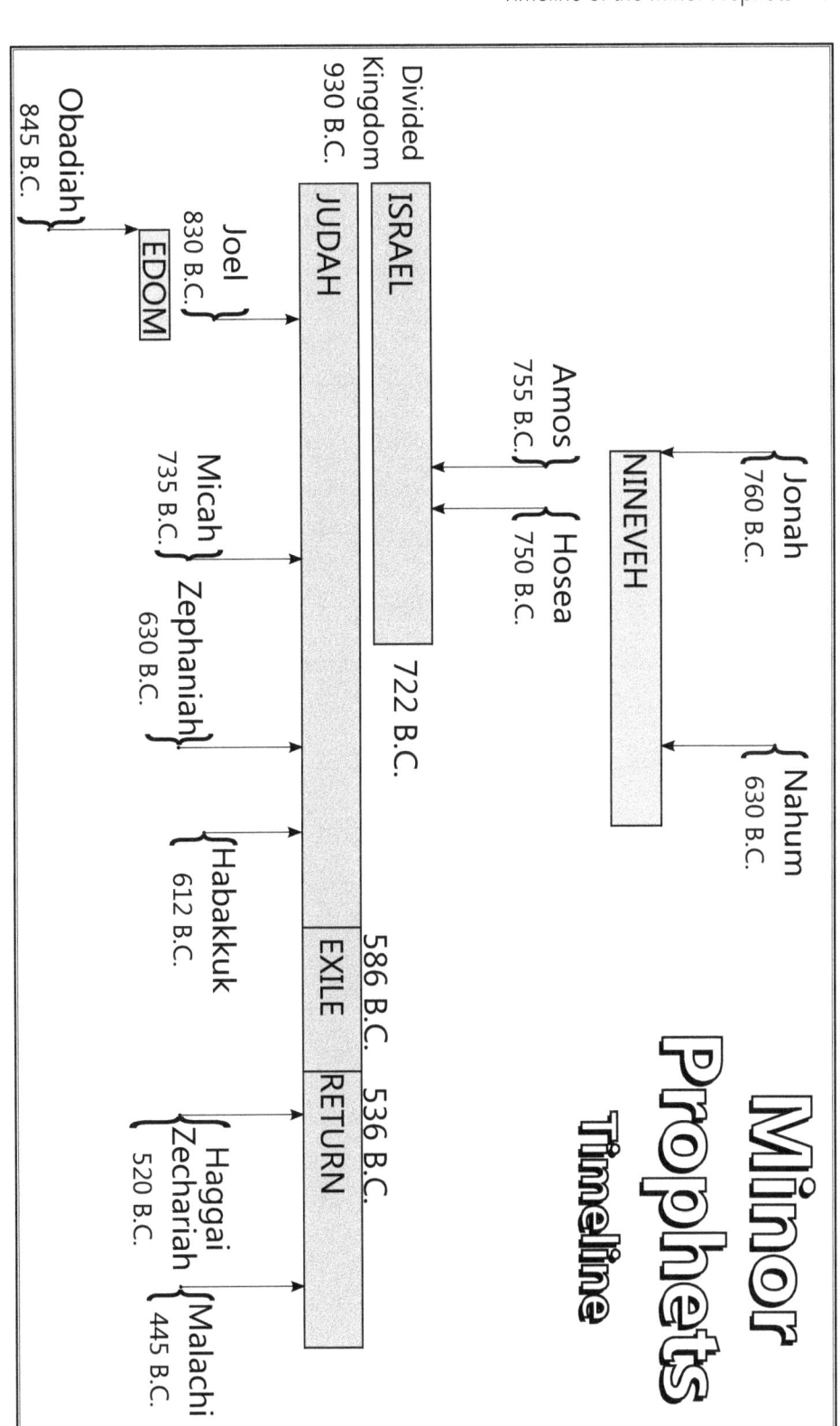

Lesson 1

THE MINOR PROPHETS

Why Are They Called Minor Prophets?

The collection of books referred to as the Minor Prophets are named this way because of the length of their writings. Don't let the name "minor" mislead you. These short books deal with serious issues of sin and disrespect for God's authority in a very serious way! Although short in length, these books are of major importance in message.

Several of the prophets recorded in the Scriptures are called oral prophets because we do not have any writings from them; Elijah, Elisha, Nathan, Ahijah, and Gad are just a few. The prophets that have left us writings bear their names and are called literary prophets.

Why Study The Minor Prophets?

A study of the books of the Minor Prophets helps us understand the overall message of the Bible. Historically, the twelve Minor Prophets' writings span a period of about 400 years of Israel and Judah's history, providing both a spiritual and historical understanding of God's chosen people. The prophets' job was to share God's mind with His people. Whenever the people strayed from God's commandments, God would send an inspired prophet to warn the people to repent. When one repents he turns away or changes directions from his sinful ways and returns to God. Repentance means to change directions. If you are heading one direction you will stop, turn, and go the other way.

What Was A Prophet?

A prophet was a man referred to as seer, man of God, servant, messenger, and watchman. A good definition for a prophet is a human mouthpiece for God. He was an authorized spokesman. Remember, Aaron was selected by God to be Moses' "prophet" because Moses needed a spokesman or "mouth" to talk to the people (Exo. 4:16; 7:1). In Deuteronomy 18:18, God later promised to raise up a Prophet and put words in his mouth. This was fulfilled in Jesus (Acts 3:22). A prophet was a man who had something to say and had to say it (Jer. 20:7-9).

At times, the prophet would *foretell* the distant future. Other times he would tell of an event that would come about in the near future. This is *forth-telling*. When a prophet spoke by God's direction, the words always came to pass. This is one of the strongest proofs that the message was from God (Isa. 42:9; 44:6-7). Generally, the prophet would try to get the peoples' attention with warnings of God's wrath that was sure to come. God's wrath would be turned away if only they would stop their sinful ways and return to God. One might call them the preacher of that time.

The prophets also foretold of God's great 'scheme of redemption' for mankind through His church. This is God's plan to rescue mankind from sin. But, most of the time, the message of the prophet addressed issues that the people were facing at that very moment in time. Although people may try to make modern-day application from some of these messages written by the ancient prophets, it is important for us to remember that the message of the prophet was always spoken to address the immediate needs of the people of that time. Understanding how God dealt with disobedience so long ago helps us understand how God deals with disobedience today. Malachi 3:6 tells us that God does not change!

Messianic Prophecies:

The New Testament writers often quoted the prophets unfolding how they foretold of Jesus' miraculous birth, death and resurrection. These are called Messianic prophecies. Jesus Himself even quoted the prophet Isaiah in Luke 4:17-21 announcing that He was the fulfillment of Isaiah 61:1-2.

How Did They Know When A Prophet Was False?

Everyone likes to hear kind words of praise and encouragement rather than hard, strong words of correction, and so did the people of ancient times. Prophets arose who told the people what they wanted to hear, not what God wanted them to know. These were called false prophets. They were not sent by God but pretended to speak for God, although they had no divine command. They told the people what they wanted to hear instead of delivering strong messages of warning and instruction. The false prophets came to "tickle the ears" of those who did not want to hear God's stern warnings. The apostle Paul wrote about this very thing.

> *For the time will come when they will not endure sound doctrine; but wanting to have their ears tickled, they will accumulate for themselves teachers in accordance to their*

own desires, and will turn away their ears from the truth and will turn aside to myths. 2 Timothy 4:3-4

The people were to reject these false prophets and not be afraid of them (Deut. 18:20-22; Jer. 28; 2 Pet. 2:1). Good and honest hearts will want to hear God's righteous message regardless of how hard or unpleasant it may be to hear. As students of the Bible, we must also be ready to hear and obey God's message for us being careful not to change the clear and simple message of the Bible.

How To Understand Each Book

To appreciate the message of each prophet we must:
1. Clearly understand the existing conditions at the time the prophet lived.
2. Understand the political, social, moral and spiritual conditions of that time.
3. Determine the audience to whom the prophet was speaking.
4. Read each prophet's book as though you were living in that day under the same conditions.

History seems to repeat itself. Solomon reminds us that there is nothing new under the sun (Eccl. 1:9). It seems to be the nature of man to become distracted by the world and get into trouble. Therefore, we should take the rich and powerful lessons recorded in the books of the Minor Prophets and be ready to make parallels by identifying the choices God would have us make when conditions of our time are similar to those of so long ago.

Things To Think About

- What lessons do the Minor Prophets teach us today? _____
  _____
  _____

- Circle one: Do we read the books of the Minor Prophets (a) to better understand Israel's history, (b) to value their warnings for us today, or (c) both?

Questions

1. Give examples of 'oral' prophets. What is the difference between an oral prophet and a literary prophet? _____
   _____
   _____

2. How many Minor Prophets are there? List them._____
_____
_____
_____

3. Why are they referred to as 'minor'? _____
_____
_____

4. Define the word prophet. What was the job of the prophet? _____
_____
_____
_____

5. Find passages where other words are used in the Bible for a prophet?
_____
_____

6. What is the difference between 'fore-telling' and 'forth-telling'? _____
_____
_____

7. What must the reader know in order to understand the true message of the minor prophet? _____
_____
_____

8. Who was a prophet to Moses and why? _____
_____
_____

9. What does the word "Messianic" mean? _____
_____
_____

10. Do we have prophets today? _____

11. Who warns us today? _____
_____

12. What are we warned about today? Why? _____
    _____
    _____

13. What happens if we do not heed the warnings? _____
    _____
    _____

14 ▪ The Minor Prophets

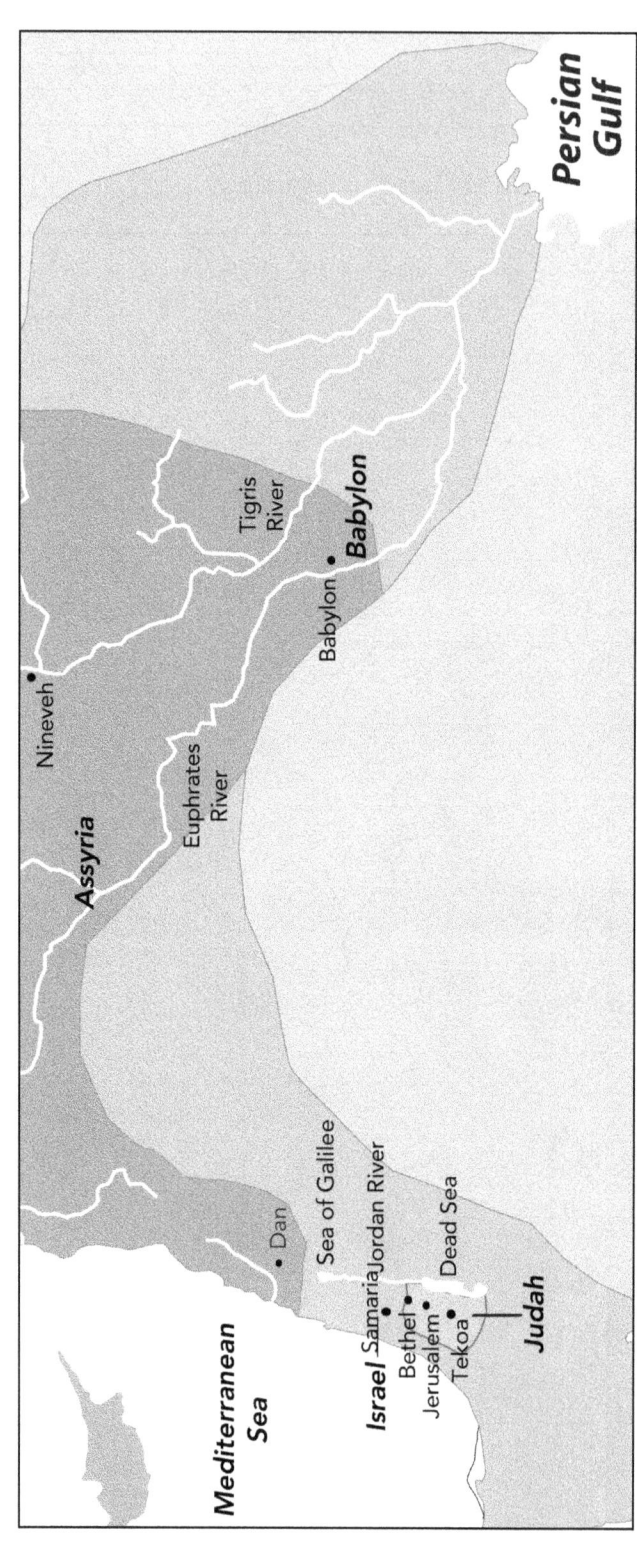

Lesson 2

HOSEA
pronounced: ho-ZEE-uh

Reading Assignment
Hosea

Who Was Hosea?

Hosea is the son of Beeri. His name means *salvation, deliverance or help*. The names Joshua and Jesus also come from the same Hebrew word. Nothing more is known about Hosea's background other than he was a prophet from God sent to Israel's ten northern tribes. It is generally believed that Hosea was a native of the north, possibly Samaria but that is not known for sure. The prophet Amos was prophesying God's message of repentance to Israel when Hosea began his ministry. It is interesting to note that during the same time Hosea and Amos were prophesying to the northern kingdom of Israel, Isaiah and Micah were prophesying to the southern kingdom of Judah.

KEY FACTS TO REMEMBER	
Where was Hosea from	Israel
To whom did he prophesy	People of Israel
Key Verses	Hosea 4:6
Memory Key	Prophet with an unfaithful wife

When Was It Written?

Hosea prophesied from 750-725 B.C. These dates coincide with the reign of the kings recorded in 1:1. These dates include the end of Israel's king, Jeroboam II's, reign through the beginning days of Judah's king, Hezekiah. It is thought that Amos had probably finished his prophesying to Israel when Hosea began his work. Hosea described pitiful conditions in Israel; political disaster, family units in ruin, wicked rulers promoting sinful living, priests encouraging open idolatry and leading the people to sin (temple whoredom). Israel was a nation crawling in the depths of sin.

What Was The Message?

The message is clearly about the righteousness of God—God is love. One of Hosea's favorite expressions is "loving-kindness." Hosea is called the prophet of love and the prophet of a broken heart.

It had been 150 years since the kingdom divided and still the people were not willing to put away their pagan idols. God had patiently and repeatedly proved His concern, love and protection to each generation of His people. To God, His people were like a wife that continued to be unfaithful to her husband. Being unfaithful is also called adultery. If a wife acts like she is married to someone whom she is not, she is committing adultery. This is a form of betrayal.

The Israelites continued in their spiritual adulterous relationship with idols. God's patience and long suffering had finally come to an end. Even Israel's priests had stopped following the law of God, allowing and even encouraging the people to practice idolatry. Hosea blamed the priests for the sinful condition of the people. God warns, *"My people are destroyed for lack of knowledge because you have rejected knowledge, I also will reject you from being priest for Me: Because you have forgotten the law of your God, I also will forget your children"* (4:6).

- Can a person be guilty of rejecting the knowledge of God today? _____
  _____
  _____

- Do you think some Bible knowledge or school knowledge is not worth learning? Explain. _____
  _____
  _____

It was time to put away Israel. Israel enjoyed much wealth at this time in history. Her prosperity and lack of respect for God caused her to turn a deaf ear to Hosea's warnings of a coming destruction. Israel was economically prosperous but spiritually bankrupt. Vulgar immoralities were introduced, worship was polluted, and oppression, murder, lying and stealing were tolerated. The people substituted the worship of Baal in the place of worship to God.

Israel's unfaithfulness could be seen in her rebellion to authority; various kings and princes had been assassinated (7:1-7) and she placed her dependence upon foreign powers instead of Jehovah (5:13; 7:11,13; 14:3, etc.). Hosea summed up Israel's spiritual condition in one word "whoredom." They had given away their stand for righteousness for the fulfillment of selfish and cheap pleasures. The spiritual condition of Israel had sunk to immoral depths.

God instructed Hosea to marry a wife of harlotry, Gomer. As a harlot, Gomer received payment for acting like she was married to men when she was not. Not long after the marriage, Gomer committed adultery against her husband Hosea. As she continued in her adulterous relationships with her lovers, the pain and hurt that she caused her husband was likened to the pain and hurt that God felt when the spiritually unfaithful Israel played the harlot with the other gods of the land. Hosea was a living example of the lesson that God wanted the children of Israel to learn. God wanted Israel, His bride, to be faithful only to Him. It was not until Hosea actually experienced the tragedy of his own marriage that he understood how to deliver God's message of love. His own experiences of sorrow, hurt and rejection helped him understand God's anguish and pain over the unfaithfulness of Israel.

- Define betray. _____
  _____
  _____

- How do you feel when you are betrayed? _____
  _____
  _____

- Define empathy. _____
  _____
  _____

- Give an example of how you can show empathy. _____
  _____
  _____

- How does one's experiences help with empathy? _____
  _____
  _____

Hosea and Gomer had three children. The names of these children represented God's coming judgments on Israel. The firstborn child was a son and God told Hosea to name him Jezreel, which means "scattered by God." This is a reference to the termination of Jehu's dynasty (1:4-5). This was the beginning of the end for the kingdom of Israel.

The second child was a daughter who was named, Lo-ruhamah, which means "without mercy." Her name was a warning that when the time came, God would not show mercy on Israel but would exact His punishment.

The third child was another son and God instructed Hosea to call him Lo-ammi, meaning "not my people." This signified God's total rejection of Israel.

The meaningful names of the children would later be changed to have opposite meanings. Their new meanings would show the mercy and eventual restoration of fellowship with God after righteous judgment.

Hosea heard from God a second time, telling him to go love Gomer again (3:1). Hosea bought her back from harlotry with the price that one would pay for a slave, 15 pieces of silver and a homer of barley. Just as Hosea redeemed, or bought back, Gomer from the slavery of sin, God was ready to redeem His people from their sin. After ignoring Hosea's message, Israel spent many years in captivity before they repented, turned back to God, and were restored to God's love and favor. Israel had "sown to the wind" and now "must reap the whirlwind" (8:7).

- In your own words, explain what it means to "sow to the wind and must reap the whirlwind." _____
_____
_____
_____

The prophecy of Hosea is a parallel between Hosea's experience with his unfaithful wife, Gomer, and God's experiences with the unfaithful nation of Israel. Israel had allowed themselves to become influenced by its heathen neighbors and had taken up idol worship instead of trusting and obeying the one true God.

Faithful to His covenant God, would not forget Israel even though she had forgotten Him. He promised to deliver her again out of bondage even as He had brought her out of Egypt so long ago. Once again the righteous relationship would be established. These promises look to the future coming of the Messiah.

The book of Hosea emphasizes divine grace would be given if the people would only repent. How many times does God pour out His blessings on His children and they forget from whom the blessings come and in turn ignore God?

Things To Think About

- Any nation who refuses to know and obey God is set for destruction because it is without morals and spiritual hope.

- Outward forms of worship alone are not sufficient to please God. He is concerned not only with what we do but why we do it. Many religious people may read the Bible and claim to believe it but unless they obey it completely, their claims are meaningless to God.

- The object of true and acceptable religion should never be to please ourselves but to please God who is the Giver of all good and righteous gifts.

- God is longsuffering. He allows man time to realize his sins and repent from them if he chooses. However, God's patience is not forever. When man realizes his sin against God, he must be quick to change and ask forgiveness. Our righteous God is quick to forgive and forget man's sins. Apparently, Israel was unwilling to repent even when they were sent as captives to Assyria. Israel, the northern kingdom, never returned to the land of promise.

Questions

1. What is the economic and political condition of Israel at the time of Hosea's message? _____
   _____
   _____

2. Who is the king of Israel at the time of Hosea's prophecy? _____
   _____
   _____

3. What does the name Hosea mean? _____
   _____
   _____

4. Who does Hosea hold mainly responsible for allowing the people to sin? _____
   _____

5. Who is Gomer and how would you describe her? _____
   _____
   _____

6. What is God's reason for having Hosea marry her? _____
   _____
   _____

7. What are the names of Gomer's three children and what do they mean?
   _____
   _____
   _____

8. What is Hosea's message to his people? _____
_____
_____

9. How does Israel respond to Hosea's words of warning? _____
_____
_____

10. Why is Hosea called the prophet of a broken heart? _____
_____
_____

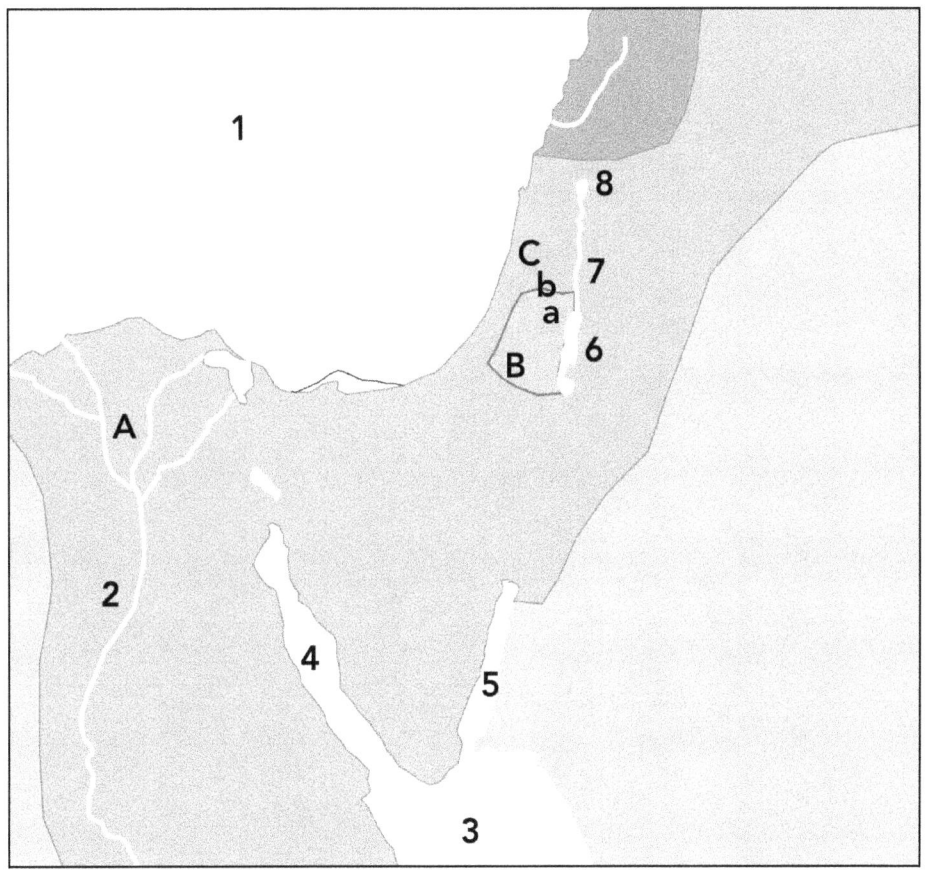

Mapping the Minor Prophets

Fill in the blanks with the letter or number that corresponds to the map locations listed below.

Bodies of Water

____ Mediterranean Sea
____ Jordan River
____ Dead Sea
____ Sea of Galilee
____ Nile River
____ Red Sea
____ Gulf of Suez
____ Gulf of Aqaba

Nations

____ Israel
____ Judah
____ Egypt

Cities

____ Jerusalem
____ Samaria

Lesson 3

JOEL

pronounced: JOH el

> **Reading Assignment**
> Joel

Who Was Joel?

KEY FACTS TO REMEMBER	
Where was Joel from	Jerusalem
To whom did he prophesy	Judah
Key Verses	Joel 2:28-32
Memory Key	Prophet of Pentecost; Locust, Drought, and Fires

Very little is known about Joel other than he was a prophet to Judah and "the son of Pethuel." Joel is a common name among the Jewish nation and means, Jehovah is God. Joel is sometimes referred to as the prophet of Pentecost because he prophesied of the coming of the Holy Spirit that was fulfilled on the day of Pentecost, fifty days after Jesus was raised from the dead in Acts 2. Joel lived in Jerusalem where the temple is ever before him (1:9, 13, 14; 2:17).

When Was It Written?

The exact writing of the book is unknown. Scholars place the book as early as 900 BC to as late as 400 BC. The best guess for the date is 830 B.C. during the reign of the wicked queen Athaliah, and the early years of Joash's reign in Judah. Even though the exact date is uncertain, God's message spoken through His prophet Joel applies to all generations.

What Was The Message?

What we do know and agree with is the theme of the book of Joel. It was unquestionably a call to repentance. Although the people of Judah had previously experienced threats from invading armies, they were not prepared for the army of locusts that swarmed over Judah, completely destroying the crops. The land was plagued by an invasion of locusts, drought and fires. Some do not believe that these were actual events, but figurative. Either way, Joel gave a description of the devastation left by invading armies. To this author, these events were real and the prophet called upon the people to repent. If they refused to repent, there would be an even stronger judgment—an invasion by the barbaric Assyrian forces from the north. The prophet warned the spiritually lazy people of Judah that anything less than their total devotion to God would result in a terrible punishment. He warned them that the 'Day of the Lord' was coming when God would make all mankind accountable for his deeds and the life he chooses to live.

- Name 3 responsibilities your parents hold you accountable. _____
_____
_____
_____
_____

In chapter 2:1, the sound of alarm was given from Zion, in Jerusalem, and the people were summoned for a general assembly. Joel pleaded with the people of Judah to pray, to fast, and to repent in order to keep God from bringing His harsh judgment upon them. The priests were told to gather all the people of the land to the house of the Lord and to cry out to the Lord (1:13-14). "For the day of the Lord is at hand and will come as destruction from God Almighty" (1:15). "Let all the inhabitants of the land tremble: for the day of the Lord is coming, for it is at hand" (2:1). The use of "the day of the Lord" in Joel refers to a day of judgment from the Lord. Sometimes it is immediate judgment (at hand) and sometimes it is the final judgment (the second coming of Christ).

- When Christ comes the second time, what will happen (1 Thes. 4:16-18; 2 Thes. 1:7-9; 2 Pet. 3:10; Matt. 25:31-46)? _____
_____
_____
_____
_____

In addition to the serious warnings to repent, Joel offered words of comfort. One day God would pour out His Spirit upon all nations. This was a promise which would be remembered when the Messiah, Christ, came and God sent His Holy Spirit in a special way to comfort and lead the followers of the Messiah (Acts 2). Joel's message was an appeal to the people, to repent and turn to God through warnings of coming judgments upon Judah for her sins, and to foretell of the glory of God's faithful people.

Like most of the prophets' messages, Joel's was an appeal from God for His people to seek Him. His message began in gloom but closed with brightness and hope for those who would listen and obey.

Things To Think About

- In Joel 2:28-32 we read about the "outpouring of the Spirit." Explain what event takes place in Acts 2:17-21 when this prophecy was fulfilled. ___
  _____
  _____
  _____
  _____

- Can you recall times when your parents or teacher warned you about something foolish you wanted to do and no matter how strong the warning was given, you were determined to follow your own way? ___
  _____
  _____

  Why do those who love you so much go to so much effort to warn you?
  _____
  _____

  It is because they really love you and want you to make right decisions. Satan wants to fool you into trusting him and believing in his lies (John 8:44; Jer. 10:23).

- To us who live in America, it may be hard to relate to the destruction God brought upon Judah during Joel's time. However, American history reveals crippling times even in our country not so very long ago. Many American's suffered economic collapse with the Stock Market crash in the 1920's. Hunger came with the droughts and 'dust bowl' of the early 1930's. Unemployment, homelessness, hopelessness and despair grew steadily during the Great Depression. These hard times might be interpreted as warnings in order to bring our nation to her knees in repentance. Our nation turned to God, but only briefly. As is man's nature, he quickly forgets the hard times and turns back to satisfying self. Can we learn from Joel that God allows mankind to suffer for his sinful pride and arrogance in order to bring about repentance? _____
  _____

- How are we like Israel? _____
  _____
  _____ Do we only turn to God during hard times and ignore Him in times of prosperity? _____
  _____

Questions

1. What does the name Joel mean? _____
   _____
   _____

2. Why is Joel sometimes referred to as "the prophet of Pentecost"? _____
   _____
   _____

3. To whom does Joel prophesy? _____
   _____
   _____

4. Who most likely was the king of Judah during Joel's prophecy? _____
   _____
   _____

5. What were some of the calamities suffered by Judah at this time (Joel 1:4, 6, 11-12, 16-18)? _____
   _____
   _____

6. Find the verses where Joel describes what would come upon Judah if they failed to repent with the suffering of the locusts, droughts and fire?
   _____
   _____

7. Using a commentary, Bible dictionary, or other resource, find two meanings of "the day of the Lord"? _____
   _____
   _____
   _____

8. In the chart below, list some consequences of continuing in sin today?

List Sin	List Consequences

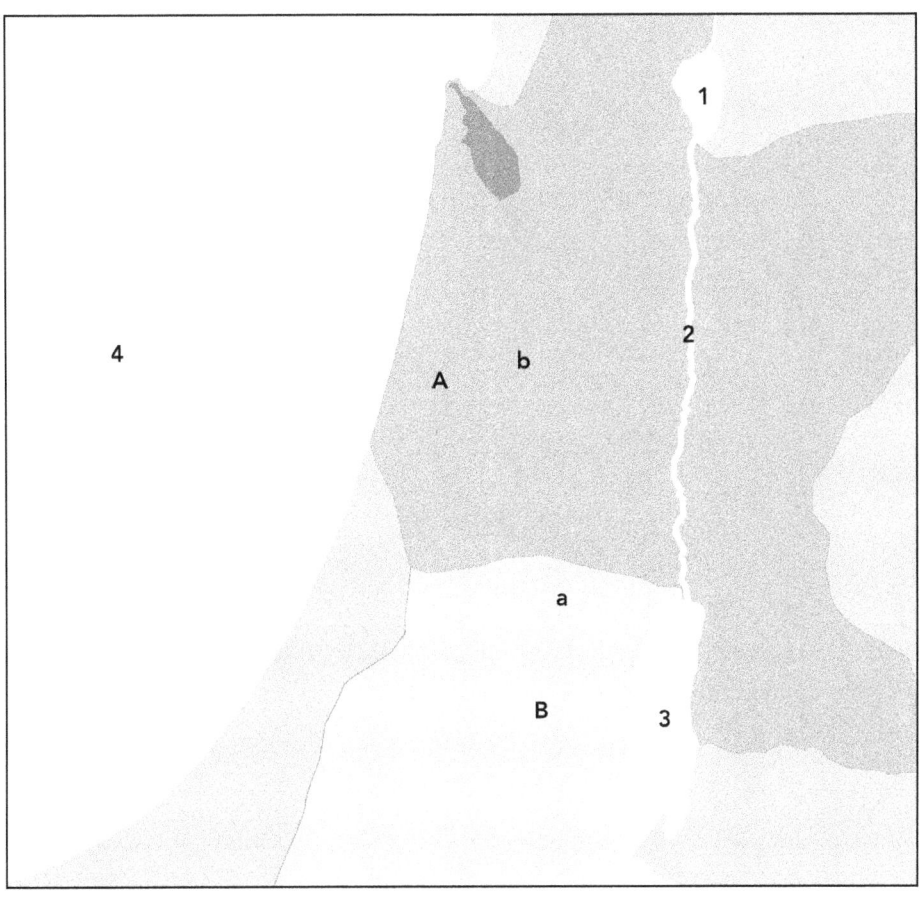

Mapping the Minor Prophets

Fill in the blanks with the letter or number that corresponds to the map locations listed below.

Bodies of Water

____ Mediterranean Sea
____ Jordan River
____ Dead Sea
____ Sea of Galilee

Nations

____ Israel
____ Judah

Cities
____ Zion (Jerusalem)
____ Samaria

Lesson 4

AMOS

pronounced: AY muhs

Reading Assignment
Amos

Who Was Amos?

The name Amos means *burden-bearer* and that certainly describes this prophet. Amos was a stern prophet of justice and righteousness.

KEY FACTS TO REMEMBER	
Where was Amos from	Tekoa of Judah
To whom did he prophesy	Israel
Key Verses	Amos 4:12
Memory Key	Prophet of Plumb line: prepare to meet your God

His home was Tekoa, a small village about 12 miles south of Jerusalem. This was a barren, rugged hill country about 18 miles west of the Dead Sea. This rugged environment helped to prepare Amos for the difficult task ahead of him as a prophet to Israel.

Amos was "a herdsman and a dresser of sycamore trees" (7:14). He took care of sheep and tended to sycamore trees. The sycamore tree that grew in Jericho (Luke 19:1-4) was found at lower elevations than Tekoa. This suggests that Amos, most likely, wandered through the wilderness in the area of the Dead Sea. The fruit of the sycamore tree is like a fig and usually eaten by only the very poorest of people. It has to be pinched or bruised before it ripes enough to be eaten.

When Was It Written?

Amos prophesied about 755 B.C. during the time of Judah's king, Uzziah, and Israel's king, Jeroboam II. God called him to prophesy toward the end of Jeroboam's reign. He prophesied two years before the earthquake. Nothing else is known about this earthquake but 400 years later people referred to it. "Then you shall flee through My mountain valley, for the mountain valley shall reach to Azal. Yes, you shall flee as you fled from the _____ in the days of _____ king of Judah. Thus the LORD my God will come, and all the saints with You," (Zech 14:5).

What Was The Message?

Israel was materially wealthy but spiritually poor. The land stunk of moral rottenness and common practices including swearing, stealing, injustice, robbery, adultery, murder, prolonged cruel and unjust treatment (2:6-12). It sounds like what we hear every day about the people of our nation on the 5 o'clock news, doesn't it? The nation was corrupt and Amos' job was to call out their evilness, warning them of the judgment that was about to happen. Jehovah laid upon Amos the heavy task of delivering His divine message to Israel. Amos says, *"A lion has roared! Who will not fear?"* (3:8)

Amos also announced God's judgment on the Gentile nations surrounding Israel. He was specific as to why God was sending His judgment upon these nations. Each judgment began with the phrase, *"Thus says the Lord, for three transgressions...and for four, I will not turn away its punishment."* God wanted them to know that He was aware of all their sins and would deliver the appropriate punishment for them. Although the Law of Moses was given only to the Hebrew nation, the Gentile nations were also under a law of God, a moral law. Romans 2:15 says there is a *"law written in their hearts."* All people of the earth are responsible to God for their own sins of not keeping God's laws. How do you write "the law of God" on your heart?

_____

_____

Amos told the Israelites to look at their neighboring Gentile cities to see the judgments God had brought upon them. Israel was just as wicked as their Gentile neighbors and they were about to suffer the same punishment. They were morally, socially and politically corrupt and in a state of religious decay, pulling farther and farther away from God.

Amos scolded the women of Samaria referring to them as *"cows of Bashan, who are on the mountain of Samaria"* (4:1). These fat, lazy Israelite women encouraged their husbands to cruelly mistreat the poor for their own silly wants and comforts. God warned them through the strong words of His prophet, Amos, that the days are coming when they would be taken away one by one with fishhooks through their jaws (4:2; Ezekiel 29:4). It is interesting to note that ancient historical writings record Assyria's use of 'fishhooks' pushed through the jaws of their captives while taking them from their homeland. This humiliating act is exactly what happened when Israel was taken into Assyrian captivity.

Since the time of Jeroboam I (1 Kings 12:25-33) idol worship had been practiced. God had sent many prophets to warn the people, but they would not repent. Amos was sent to a nation that was so confident in itself that it removed God out of their lives. God sent famine, drought, blight and mildew, locusts, pestilence, and overthrew cities (4:6-11). After each judgment, God remarked, *"You have not returned to me."*

- After each judgment or punishment, why do you think the people did not return to God? _____
  _____

- Have you learned from mistakes you have made in the past? _____
  Name some: _____
  _____
  _____

It was too late for Israel; there was nowhere to run from God's wrath. Since these strong punishments would not cause the people to return to God, Amos warned that they should *"prepare to meet your God O Israel"* i (4:12). The people were so wicked but Amos still hoped some would turn back to righteousness so that a remnant might be saved.

God showed Amos what judgments He wanted to bring upon Israel in five visions. Amos pleaded with God to spare Israel, after each one (7:1-10). In the visions he saw:

1. Locusts- they would eat up the crops and the people would starve. Amos prayed for God to forgive them so God changed His mind and didn't send the judgment of locusts.

2. Fire- it would be a consuming fire that would destroy both land and water. Again Amos prayed and God did not send this judgment.

3. Plumb line- a plumb line is a line to which a weight is attached to determine if something is straight. The vision was the Lord standing on a wall holding a plumb line in His hand. Sadly, the people were out of line with God's standard and He wanted to tear down the wall that had become crooked.

At this point in time, Amos was accused of trying to start a rebellion against the king's authority. This accusation came from Amaziah, the idolatrous high priest of Bethel (7:10-17). Amaziah was so upset that he told Amos to go back to Judah, never to come to Israel again. Amos argued that it was God who took him from his flocks and his work with the sycamore trees, telling him to, *"Go, prophesy to my people Israel."* Amos was not a paid prophet like Amaziah, but a prophet God sent to deliver a strong message. Because of Amaziah's attempt to run Amos out of Israel, his family would be cursed, his wife would become a harlot, his sons and daughters would be killed by the sword, his land divided and Amaziah would die in a foreign land (7:16-17).

Visions continue:

4. Basket of Summer Fruit- the time of mercy had now passed because Israel was ripe for destruction. The Lord would not pass by them any more.

5. The Destruction of Israel- Amos saw the Lord standing by the altar saying, *"I will destroy the house of Israel from the face of the earth; Yet I will not utterly destroy the house of Jacob."* (9:8)

Amos did his job by exposing the peoples' sins. He pointed out that elaborate offerings could not be a substitute for righteousness (5:21-24; John 4:24; Rom 12:1-2). Amos condemned the judges of Israel for their cruelty of the poor. He also condemned Israel for its lack of reverence in their service to God. Israel didn't want to believe the warnings Amos was preaching.

Sadly, Israel had become like the other nations since it had lost its special relationship with God. Now God would destroy the nation of Israel but not completely (9:8). An invitation to repent was offered by the prophet to the remnant but not to the entire nation of Israel. If the sinner would seek God and turn away from his idolatry, he would live. The prophet warned that death and danger were surely coming for many, and fear would overtake those who were not killed in the judgment of God (6:9-10). This judgment was described as destruction that was complete and no one would escape.

The book ends with a ray of hope (9:11-15; Acts 15:15-18). The promise of God to preserve a "faithful remnant" was the ray of hope to those who repented and put their trust in God even in the difficult times to come.

In summary, the prophecy of Amos looked to the future with the promise of the Messiah. God promised to *"raise up the tabernacle of David which has fallen down, and repair its damages; I will raise up its ruins, and rebuild it as in the days of old"* (9:11). This meant the nation of Israel had fallen because of sin, but God would raise it up in the future as the church—the kingdom of Christ. The Gentiles would also be allowed to be a part of this rebuilt tabernacle. This represented a major change in the new covenant of Christ to include Gentiles (9:11).

Things To Think About

- Is being religious enough? _____
  _____ Does it matter how we worship God as long as we get it done?
  _____

- When people become wealthy and comfortable, like the "cows of Bashan" and get too much 'stuff,' they sometime forget that God is the Giver of all good and great gifts. People tend to develop a self-reliant attitude. What are some of the dangers in gaining wealth and 'stuff' and not learning how

to manage them? _____
_____ How do you handle the blessings
God has given you? _____
_____
_____

Questions

1. What does Amos do for a living? _____
   _____

2. What is his job as a prophet? _____
   _____

3. Where did Amos live, Judah or Israel? _____

4. To which nation is he sent to deliver God's message? _____

5. Do you think your sins can be hidden? _____
   _____

6. What does history tell us about how Assyria used the fishhook? ___
   _____
   _____

7. What is a plumb line? _____
   _____

8. What should be our plumb line? _____
   _____

9. Does God show His patience? _____ How? _____
   _____
   _____

10. Who is Amaziah? _____
    _____
    _____

11. What does Amos prophesy would happen to Amaziah and his family?
    _____
    _____

12. Is God aware of my every sin? _____ Will He deliver punishment for my unrepented sin? _____

13. What is the hope that God offers to His rebellious people? _____
    _____

    What are the conditions of that hope? _____
    _____
    _____

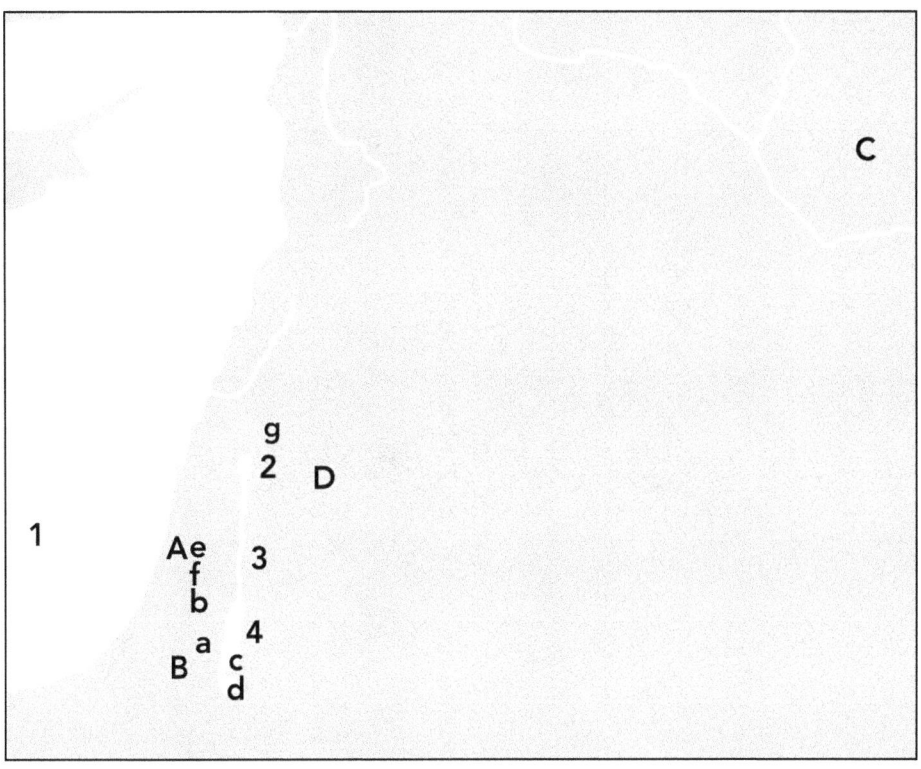

Mapping the Minor Prophets

Fill in the blanks with the letter or number that corresponds to the map locations listed below.

Bodies of Water

____ Mediterranean Sea
____ Jordan River
____ Dead Sea
____ Sea of Galilee

Nations

____ Israel
____ Judah
____ Assyria
____ Bashan

Cities

____ Jerusalem
____ Samaria

____ Tekoa
____ Bethel

____ Dan
____ Sodom
____ Gomorrah

Lesson 5

OBADIAH
pronounced: oh-buh-DY-uh

Reading Assignment
Obadiah

Who Was Obadiah?

The name Obadiah means Servant of Jehovah. Nothing is known of this prophet except what is learned from this prophecy. This is the shortest book in the Old Testament. It is a prophecy of doom upon the Edomites because of their false pride.

KEY FACTS TO REMEMBER

Where was Obadiah from	Not sure, probably Judah
Of whom did he prophesy	Edomites, bitter enemies of Israel
Key Verses	Obadiah 1:8
Memory Key	God will destroy prideful Edom; Be your brother's keeper

When Was It Written?

Scholars disagree on the date of the writing of Obadiah; however, strong arguments seem to favor the earlier date of circa 845 B.C. (circa = an approximate date)

Who Were The Edomites?

Remember the Edomites were descendants of Esau and were always bitter enemies of the Israelites, descendants of Esau's brother Jacob. This strife began before the birth of the twin boys, Esau and Jacob, while they were in their mother's womb (Gen 25:22-26). God selected the second son, Jacob, to be the lineage for His chosen people, Israel. Esau was a rebellious and profane man, and God rejected him. Hatred existed between Esau and Jacob throughout their lives.

- How do you think the parents of Jacob and Easu felt about their kids not liking each other? _____
_____
_____

The country of Edom was a range of rocky mountains east and south of the Dead Sea. It was a narrow strip of land extending about 100 miles north and south and about 20 miles east and west. The Edomites would go out on raiding parties, attack their victims, then retreat to their strongholds high up in the rocky cliffs where they felt protected from their enemies. They were also known to charge fees to the travelers who passed through their land, or else there would be consequences. They were true "bullies."

Conflict between the two nations, Israel and Edom, began at the time of the exodus (Num 20:14-21). During the reign of Jehoram, a king of Judah, Edom revolted (2 Kgs 8:20-22). Eventually, the Edomites were overcome by the Nabataeans and driven from their land around 300 B.C. Around the close of the second century B.C. the nation of Edom was completely dissolved.

What Was The Message?

The prophet Obadiah had a vision from God announcing judgment upon Edom. The Edomites were a prideful, arrogant people who would come down out of their "nest" from high up in the rocky cliffs, swoop down like eagles upon their enemies, retreat to their cliffs for safety then boast that their enemies could never reach them. Edom showed her cruel hatred for Israel, her brother, when Israel was under attack and Edom would not lift a hand to help her fight. They should have been a protector of their brother, Israel. Obadiah warned that the deeds of the Edomites would "return on their own head", and proclaimed, "As you have done, so will it be done to you." (1:15)

While the prophets of Judah and Israel shouted for the people to repent and return to the Lord, Obadiah prophesied a different judgment on the nation of Edom. God would not completely destroy Judah, but Edom would be completely destroyed, never to return or even exist as a nation again.

The book of Obadiah teaches that God's displeasure and judgment rests upon those who rejoice in the calamity of others.

- Discuss instances when you have witnessed someone rejoicing in anothers calamity. _____
_____
_____

Things To Think About

- The land that ancient Edom occupied is now modern Petra, in the country of Jordan. It is a beautiful site to visit. The name Petra is from the Greek word "petra", meaning, "rock." When entering the red-rose city of Petra on horseback through a narrow opening, one is overwhelmed by the Nabataeans' rock-cut temple of El-Khazne. Numerous rock formations, rock-hewn temples and tombs in the surrounding cliffs of the canyons adorn the area.

Questions

1. Of whom did the prophet Obadiah prophesy? _____

2. How are the two nations of Edom and Israel related? _____

3. Which of the twins had God chosen for the Savior's lineage? _____

4. What does it mean to be your brother's keeper? _____

5. What are some ways to look out for your brother? _____

6. Why does Edom think they are untouchable? _____

7. Selfishness, greed, and pride would best describe which nation of people?

   a. Selfishness. "The people will _____ him who _____ grain, but _____ will be on the head of him who _____ it," (Pro. 11:26). Give an example of selfishness from your

life and its effect on others. _____
_____
_____

b. Greed. "So are the ways of everyone who is _____ for gain; it takes away the _____ of its owners," (Pro. 1:19). Give an example of greed from your life and its effect on others. __
_____
_____

c. Pride. "A man's _____ will bring him _____, but the _____ in spirit will retain _____," (Pro. 29:23). Give an example of pride from your life and its effect on others. _____
_____
_____

Below is a picture of Petra.

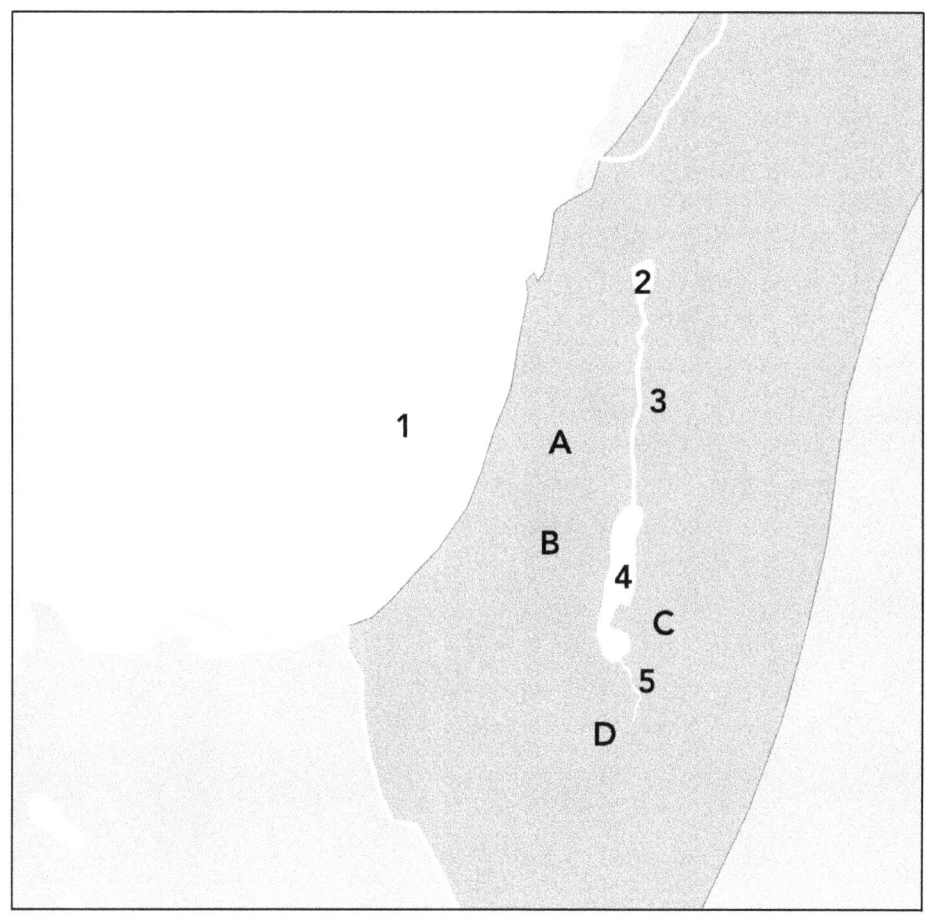

Mapping the Minor Prophets

Fill in the blanks with the letter or number that corresponds to the map locations listed below.

Bodies of Water

____ Mediterranean Sea
____ Jordan River
____ Dead Sea
____ Sea of Galilee
____ Zered River

Nations

____ Israel
____ Judah
____ Edom
____ Moab

Lesson 6

JONAH
pronounced: JOH-nuh

Reading Assignment
Jonah

Who Was Jonah?

KEY FACTS TO REMEMBER

Where was Jonah from	Israel
To whom did he prophesy	People of Nineveh of Assyria
Key Verses	Jonah 1:1-2
Memory Key	Swallowed by a great fish

The name Jonah means dove. He was the son of Amittai and his home was Gath-hepher, a village in the land of Zebulun. This would make him a prophet from Galilee.[1]

When Was It Written?

Jonah prophesied in Israel during the days of Jeroboam II around 760 B.C. (2 Kings 14:23-25).

What Was The Message?

The book of Jonah is unique from the other books of prophecy in that it does not contain any prophecies, only the message of Jonah to the Ninevites. The message is God accepts men everywhere who will repent. Jonah's selfishness was equal to the selfishness of the Israelites who did not think ALL men were worthy of salvation.

God told his prophet Jonah to go to the great city Nineveh and tell the people to repent. Jonah would rather God destroyed all the people of Nineveh than to give them an opportunity to hear God's word and repent because the people of Nineveh were the cruel enemies of Israel. Jonah decided to run away from his task and boarded a ship going to Tarshish.

---

1   Note the mistake of the Pharisees in John 7:52, "...Search and look, for 'no prophet had arisen out of Galilee.'" Apparently the uninspired Pharisee didn't remember Jonah.

This was the complete opposite direction of Nineveh. How silly to think a man could hide from God. God caused a great wind to arise and toss the ship about. The storm was so fierce that the sailors were afraid their ship would be broken up by the waves and be destroyed. The captain told everyone on board to pray for their gods to rescue them from the violent storm. When the sailors looked for Jonah to have him pray, they found him asleep in the belly of the ship. Jonah told the sailors that he was the reason for the storm and in order to save the ship and all that was aboard, the sailors should throw him overboard. The sailors didn't really want to do this but finally they listened to Jonah and threw him overboard; immediately the storm stopped. Don't you think the sailors might have gained a lot of respect for the awesome power of Jonah's God through this experience?

God did not allow Jonah to drown in the sea but rescued him by preparing a large fish to swallow him. For three days and three nights Jonah was trapped inside the belly of the great fish. Amongst the darkness, with seaweed wrapped around his head, the putrid smells, and the rocking motion of the waves as the great fish swam through the deep, Jonah prayed for mercy. God heard His prophet and had the great fish to spit Jonah out on dry ground. Now Jonah, although still not happy about his instructions to preach to the people of Nineveh, went directly and shouted the warning of God's hand of destruction that was to come upon them in 40 days if the people did not repent.

The people of Nineveh believed Jonah's warnings from God and did repent. The king sent out a decree to the entire city for all the people to fast and cry mightily to God that He might change His mind and not destroy them. God saw their works that they repented from their evil and withdrew His plan of destruction.

Nineveh's repentance did not make Jonah happy. In fact, he was so upset that he asked God to kill him. Jonah went outside the city, sat, and waited to see what God was going to do to Nineveh. As he waited, God allowed a gourd vine to grow and provide shade from the hot sun for Jonah. Jonah was very thankful for the shade but during the night God sent a worm to damage the plant and the gourd vine died. The selfish prophet was angry again and wanted to die. God pointed out to Jonah that his pity for the dead plant was similar to the pity he should have had in his heart for the people of Nineveh. He had not made or caused the plant to grow yet he was sad when it was gone. On the other hand, Jonah had no pity in his heart for the people with souls whom God had created and desired to repent.

History

To get a better understanding of the events of the time, it is important to understand a few facts about Nineveh. Genesis 10:9-11 tells us that Nimrod was its founder. In 900 B.C. Assyria rose to be a world power. Nineveh, the capital of the Assyrian Empire, was located on the east bank of the Tigris River. This was a nation that carried the northern kingdom of Israel into captivity, never to be restored. The great city of Nineveh fell in 612 B.C. It was referred to as "that great city" because of its size. The population was estimated to be around 600,000. Nineveh was destroyed by the military alliance of the Medes, Babylonians and Sythians in 612 B.C.

Things To Think About

- Interestingly, there are three interpretations of the book: the mythical, allegorical and historical. Of course the mythical view is that the book is an elaborate fairy tale. Unbelievers deny that a fish swallowed Jonah; they consider the book as a myth, or fictitious. However, Jesus regarded the account as a historical fact. The word 'whale' means great fish or sea monster. Many sea monsters have been found large enough to swallow a man—just visit a museum of natural history and see for yourself.

- The allegorical view is that the story is an allegory of Israel's captivity, repentance and restoration to its land. The historical view is that all the events actually occurred. In Matthew 12:39-41 and Luke 11:29-32 we read, "Jonah was three days and three nights in the belly of the great fish, so will the Son of Man be three days and three nights in the heart of the earth." Since these are Jesus' words referring to His death, burial and resurrection, the historical view is the only view that can be accepted by those who believe Jesus is the Christ the Son of God. This was divine evidence of Jonah's mission to Nineveh.

- Consider the impact of all the first-hand events and stories these sailors must have told to many people as they traveled from place to place; the sudden, terrible storm, Jonah telling them he was running from God, the storm immediately stopping when he was tossed overboard, a great fish appearing from the deep to swallow him and then seeing or hearing about Jonah being alive and preaching about his God to the people of Nineveh a few days later. Do you think a story like Jonah's could travel the world quickly? How? _____
_____

- What a comfort to realize that God is near and He is in control. Even when Jonah was in the belly of the great fish, deep in the ocean, God heard the prayers of His servant.

Questions

1. What is the name of the city God tells Jonah to go warn? _____
_____

2. This city is the capital of what country? _____

3. Why is Nineveh called a "great city"? _____
_____

4. Jonah tried to hide from God. Can you hide from God? _____.
   Consider things you hide from parents, preachers, elders, etc.? _____
_____
_____

5. Why do the sailors throw Jonah overboard during the storm? _____
_____
_____

6. How many days is Jonah inside the belly of the great fish? _____
_____

7. Describe what you think the 3 days and 3 nights might have been like.
_____
_____

8. How is Jonah delivered from the sea? _____
_____
_____

9. What is significant in the New Testament about "3 days in the belly of a fish" (Matt. 12:40)? _____
_____
_____

10. What lesson should be learned in Jonah's attitude about the plant in contrast to saving souls from destruction? _____
_____
_____

11. Why would Jonah be so upset about Nineveh's repentance? _____
_____

Are you ever upset with the repentance of others? If so, what does that say about your judgment of others? _____
_____
_____

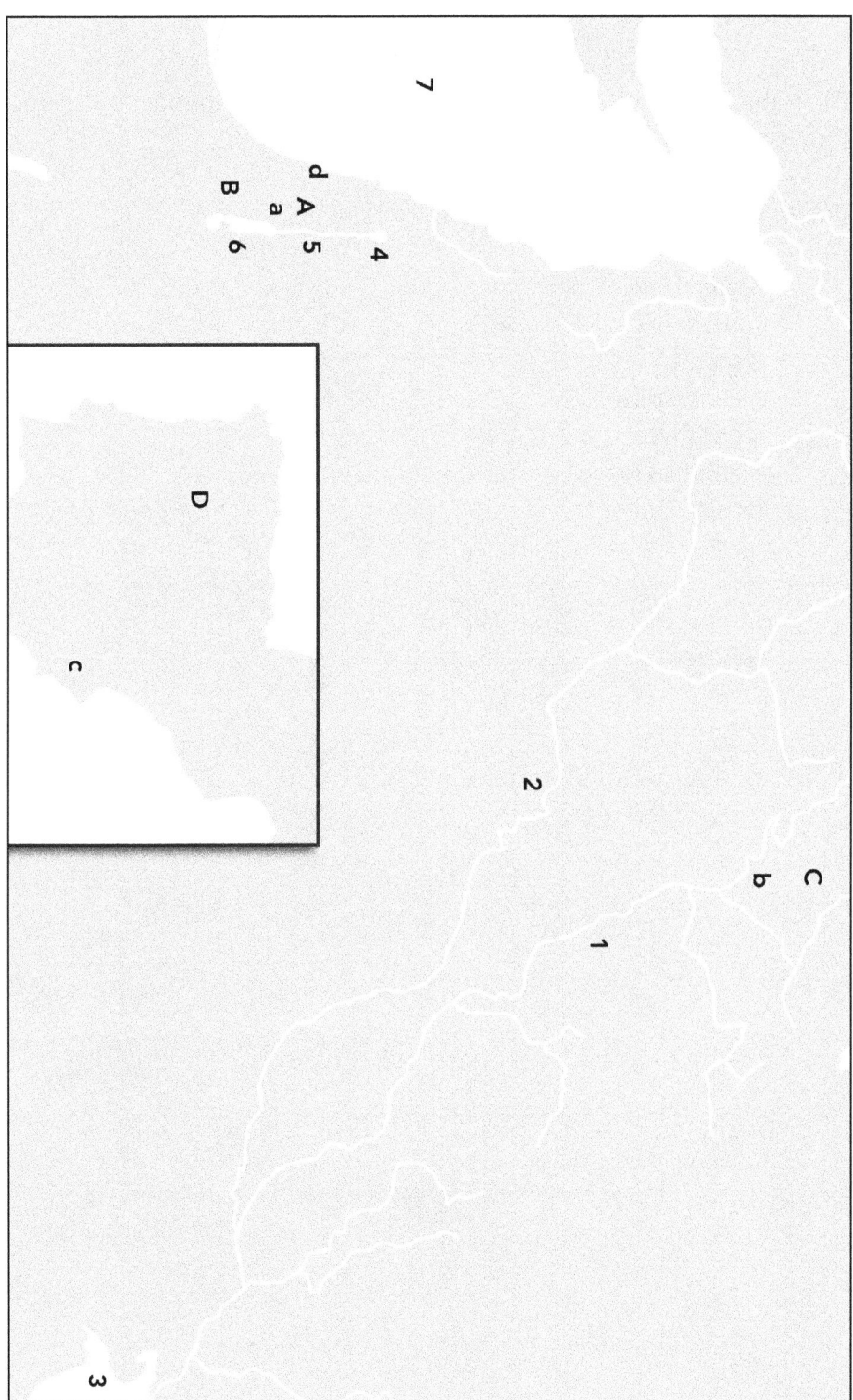

Mapping the Minor Prophets

Fill in the blanks with the letter or number that corresponds to the map locations listed below.

Bodies of Water

____ Mediterranean Sea
____ Jordan River
____ Dead Sea
____ Sea of Galilee
____ Tigris River
____ Euphrates River
____ Persian Gulf

Nations

____ Israel
____ Judah
____ Assyria
____ Spain

Cities

____ Jerusalem   ____ Tarshish
____ Nineveh   ____ Joppa

Lesson 7

MICAH
pronounced: MAI-kuh

Reading Assignment
Micah

Who Was Micah?

Micah's name means *Who is like Jehovah*? His home was Moresh-eth-gath about 20 miles southwest of Jerusalem.

KEY FACTS TO REMEMBER

Where was Micah from	Judah
To whom did he prophesy	To Judah about Israel
Key Verses	Micah 6:6-8
Memory Key	The country prophet; "a day in court"

The Holy Scriptures record nothing of Micah's call to prophesy or his personal experiences. Like Amos, Micah was a simple countryman. He was a prophet to the poor and downtrodden. He forcefully and fearlessly spoke about the evils of his day and why they were so unfair. This was in stark contrast to the prophet Isaiah who was a city prophet of high social standing and a counselor to kings.

When Was It Written?

Micah and Isaiah prophesied to Judah during the reigns of Jotham, Ahaz and Hezekiah. The kingdom of Israel still existed under the reigns of Israel's kings, Pekah and Hoshea. This places the dates of Micah's prophecy between 735-700 B.C. Under King Jotham, splendid luxury abounded, but under King Ahaz, Judah was forced to pay tribute to Assyria in which both the rich and poor of Judah suffered. Idolatry had become acceptable practice in Judah and King Hezekiah attempted to turn Judah back to righteousness. Unfortunately, conditions only became worse (II Chron 29-31).

What Was The Message?

Micah's message was clear. He encouraged Judah to look at the judgments upon Israel so they might avoid the same wrath of God. They were found guilty of their sins and their sins would not go unpunished. Micah was so distressed in the message God had given him to deliver against Judah that he prophesied barefoot, stripped to the waist and made mournful shrieking sounds like an owl. Instead of Judah acting like a child of God, it had become like God's enemies in criminal acts against the innocent, weak, women and children. Even the leaders of the people were involved in unlawful activities. Instead of leading the people to righteousness, they were leading them into sinfulness. The leaders and people didn't want to hear Micah's strong message of repentance. They would rather listen to the comforting approving message of the false prophets.

- Do you always "hear" and "listen" to the wise words of parents, elders, and preachers? _____

- Think about some wise counsel you have been told, but decided to do what you wanted. List the advice/command and the outcome.
  1. _____
  2. _____
  3. _____

These were trying times and there was a threat of invasion that added to the unrest. The Assyrian King Sennacherib captured and claimed 46 cities of Judah. The pleading and trusting in God by good king Hezekiah along with the fearless preaching of Isaiah and Micah saved Jerusalem from Assyria. Micah told Judah that there were consequences for their sins and reminded them that their evil state would result in their oppressive captivity to Babylon. It is interesting to note that at the time of Micah's prophecy, Babylon was not yet an independent power and would not become one until 100 years later. Assyria was the world power at this time.

Micah *fore-tells* that Jesus would be born in Bethlehem 700 years before it happened. This makes this book a Messianic prophecy. No one could have predicted these events with such accuracy unless Micah was inspired by the Holy Spirit to predict them. The fulfillment of prophecy is one of the strongest proofs that the Bible is from the mind of God. The hope that comes with the Messianic prophecy would only be realized after God's judgment was delivered. Always remember that there are consequences to our every decision—either for good or for evil. It is a wise person who follows God's ways.

Consequences of Good and Bad Actions

List some consequences that could result from the following actions. Be sure to consider how each decision affects those who know you.

Cheating on a test	
Lying to parents	
Viewing inappropriate material on the internet	
Attending Bible study and worship assemblies	
Obeying your parents in the Lord	
Helping the handicap, shut-in, or elderly	

The Lord asked His people what He had done to make them tire of receiving His blessings. Why didn't they care if they pleased Him or not? The people were just going through the motions of worship when their heart and thoughts were somewhere else. God was disgusted by their offers of sacrifice because no sooner had they offered up their sacrifices to Him, then they would go back to cheating, stealing, lying and abusing their neighbors. In fact, their society had become so wicked that they were warned not to trust their neighbor, friend, wife or even child. A society so corrupt demanded God's wrath and Micah was screaming the warnings as to what was coming because of their wickedness.

- Do you care if you please God? _____
- Are you just going thru the motions of worship? _____
- Are your thoughts during worship ever somewhere else? _____
- Do any of your actions disgust God? _____

There was also some hope in Micah's message. For Judah, there would be a faithful remnant that would again love and respect the Lord. For us, God's mercy gives an opportunity to repent since He does not stay angry with us forever (7:18-19). Micah tells man just what God requires from him. "He has shown you O man what is good: and what does the Lord require of you but to do justly to love mercy and to walk humbly with your God." (6:8)

Things To Think About

- People want to hear words of comfort and approval and are drawn to the smooth words of false prophets like those of Micah's day. Just because someone claims to be delivering the word of God, does not mean that he really is. How do you determine if what someone is telling you is from God or a lie from Satan? _____
_____
_____

- Micah was a strong preacher delivering a very unpopular message from God; a message of judgment because God's people refused to repent and turn back to Him. What do you think today's preachers should be preaching? _____
_____ Do you think they should only tell us what is sweet to our ears? _____ Or, should they preach the whole Truth including the hard things we don't want to hear? ___
_____

Questions

1. To whom is Micah prophesying? _____
_____

2. Who is the other prophet preaching at this same time to the city people?
_____

3. Who is the world power at the time of this prophecy? _____
_____

4. Why was Jerusalem spared under King Hezekiah's leadership? _____
_____
_____

5. Who is the world power that takes Judah into captivity about 100 years after Micah's warning? _____

6. God tells man how He wants us to behave. Write down and memorize Micah 6:8. _____
_____
_____

7. In your own words tell what a Messianic prophecy is. _____
_____
_____
_____

8. Why is this important to know? _____
_____
_____
_____

Mapping the Minor Prophets

Fill in the blanks with the letter or number that corresponds to the map locations listed below.

Bodies of Water

____ Mediterranean Sea
____ Sea of Galilee
____ Dead Sea
____ Jordan River

Nations

____ Judah
____ Assyria
____ Israel

Cities

____ Bethlehem
____ Samaria
____ Moresheth-gath (20 mi. SW of Jerusalem)
____ Jersusalem

Lesson 8

NAHUM

pronounced: NAY-huhm

Reading Assignment
Nahum

Who Was Nahum?

KEY FACTS TO REMEMBER

Where was Nahum from	Judah
To whom did he prophesy	Oppressed Judah about the coming destruction of Nineveh of Assyria
Key Verses	Nahum 1:8
Memory Key	The doom of Nineveh; flood of Tigris River

Nahum's name means consolation or console. He was from Elkosh, an area that archaeologists still have not been able to locate. Some think it was the site of Capernaum, others guess it might be in Assyria, but the Bible does not tell us so we will leave Elkosh's location as unknown. What we do know is that Nahum was to prophesy to the oppressed people of Judah, about Nineveh's judgment, offering them comfort.

When Was It Written?

The date of Nahum's prophecy is thought to be between two events; the fall of No-amon, the Egyptian city known as Thebes by the king of Assyria around 663 B.C. (3:8) and when the Medes and Chaldeans destroyed Nineveh in 612 B.C. [1] Therefore we will narrow the date to the time between 650 and 612 B.C.

What Was The Message?

Two of the Minor Prophets delivered God's messages about Nineveh, the capital of Assyria, the great and wicked force from the north; they were Jonah (780 B.C.) and Nahum about 150 years later. Remember Jonah's message was one of mercy if the wicked people of Nineveh would repent and they did repent. Nahum's message was one of doom for the mighty

---

[1] The British Museum tablet #21,901 furnishes some interesting information about the early battles of this city.

and cruel Assyrians. Together, these two prophets illustrate God's method of dealing with the nations; God extends His grace with the opportunity to repent and punishment for those who refuse to repent. It is interesting to note that Nahum did not mention the sins of Judah but dealt only with the doom of Assyria and God's victory over them.

Assyria was thought to be one of the most brutal and cruel nations of ancient times. Nahum said about Nineveh, "Woe to the bloody city! It is all full of lies and robbery" (3:1). It was proven time and again in the invasion of Israel:

1. In 722 B.C. they conquered the northern kingdom of Israel (2 Kings 17:6).

2. In 701 B.C. they led an invasion attack against Judah during King Hezekiah's reign (2 Kings 18:13-18).

Nahum foretold of the certain downfall of Nineveh, the capital of Assyria. Her city walls would be destroyed from the flooding of the Tigris River (2:6). Nineveh was not concerned about this because her walls were 50 feet thick and 100 feet high. History records that for a period of 3 months the Babylonian army used battering rams to weaken the walls. A great rain came and the Tigris River flooded collapsing a weakened section of the wall. Through this breach, the Babylonians entered the city to burn and utterly destroy it. This is the fulfillment of God's prophecy that the walls would be destroyed and that the Babylonian army came through like "an overflowing flood" (1:8) and destroyed everything else.

The message was clear and encouraging to Judah. The Lord would bring judgment upon sinful Nineveh but would spare Judah. As always, God's prophecy was fulfilled and the wicked city of Nineveh was totally wiped away (3:17). Its destruction was so complete that the site of the city was forgotten. When Alexander the Great fought the famous battle of Arbela in 331 B. C., almost 300 years later, near the site of Nineveh, he did not know a city had ever been there.[2] Nineveh stood as a grave of ruins until it was first explored by C.J. Rich in A.D. 1820 and excavated for the first time by Paul Botta in 1824.[3]

Things to think about

- Although the message of Nahum was for the people of his day, God's people today should still trust in the same God who rules over the affairs and nations of men and calls all men to account for their actions (2 Cor 5:10). Should we pray for our nation? _____. For

---

2 *Halley's Handbook*, pg 370
3 M.R. Wilson, "Nineveh," *Major Cities of the Biblical World*, R.K. Harrison, ed., 182.

what should we pray? _____

- God's faithful must be patient, trusting in the goodness and justice of their Lord, who has promised to protect the faithful and punish the wicked. Learning to "Wait on the Lord" is not always an easy thing to do but man must learn that God knows when and what is best for His children. We only think we know.

Questions

1. What is the meaning of the name Nahum? _____
   _____

2. Where is he from and what do you know about this city? _____
   _____
   _____

3. Who is another minor prophet that prophesied about Nineveh? _____
   _____

4. What is the message of the book? _____
   _____
   _____

5. How do you know that Nahum's prophecy was fulfilled? _____
   _____
   _____

6. Why is Nineveh called "the bloody city?" What do you know about its people? _____
   _____
   _____

7. Read Nahum 1:2 and in your own words tell what it means that "God is jealous and takes vengeances"? _____
   _____
   _____
   _____

58 ◂ The Minor Prophets

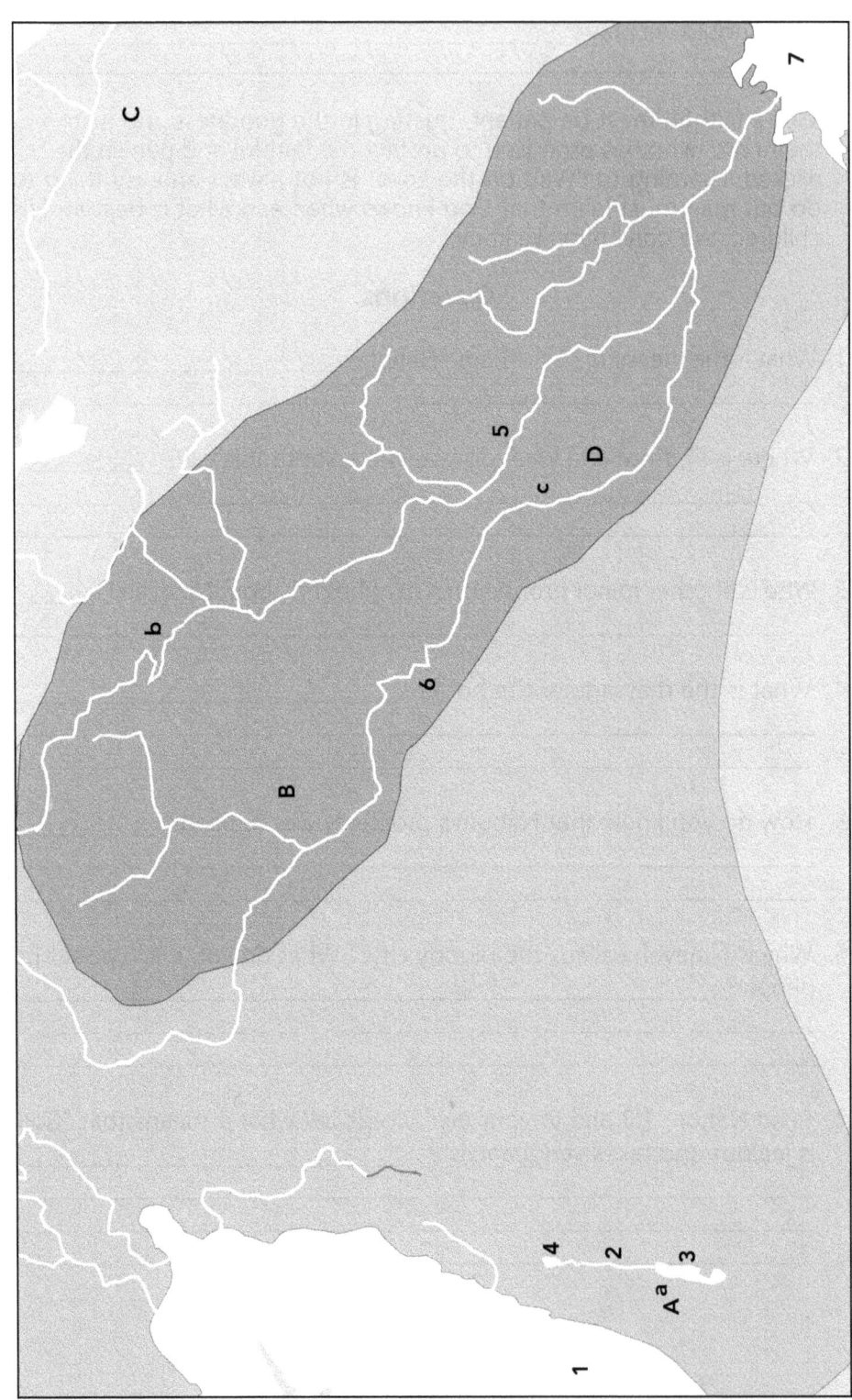

Mapping the Minor Prophets

Fill in the blanks with the letter or number that corresponds to the map locations listed below.

Bodies of Water

____ Sea of Galilee
____ Persian Gulf
____ Tigris River
____ Mediterranean Sea
____ Dead Sea
____ Euphrates River
____ Jordan River

Nations

____ Mede
____ Chaldea (Babylon)
____ Assyrian Empire
____ Judah

Cities

____ Jerusalem
____ Babylon
____ Nineveh

HABAKKUK
pronounced: huh-BAK-uhk

Reading Assignment
Habakkuk

Who was Habakkuk?

KEY FACTS TO REMEMBER

Where was Habakkuk from	Judah
To whom did he prophesy	Judah about the coming destruction of the Babylonians
Key Verses	Habakkuk 2:20
Memory Key	Wherever evil is found, its own destruction will follow

Habakkuk is an unusual Hebrew name that comes from the verb *embrace*. This name probably means one who embraces or one who clings. The name suggests that Habakkuk was one who took another to his heart like one who comforts a weeping child. The name fits as we read how Habakkuk chose to cling to God regardless of what happened to his nation. The Bible does not mention very much about this prophet other than his name and that he was a man of strong faith (2:4). His occupation and hometown are unknown. However, from Habakkuk's strong delivery of God's message to Judah, much about this remarkable servant of God is revealed. This prophet of Judah is probably prophesying at the same time as Jeremiah. Habakkuk's prayer in the last half of the book is one of the grandest prayers in the Bible (Hab. 3).

When was it written?

Delivering God's words at the same time as the Prophet Jeremiah, Habakkuk's message to Judah was thought to have been written during the time of wicked King Jehoiachin's reign, around 612-606 BC.

What was the Message?

The ten northern tribes of Israel had already fallen into Assyrian captivity when Habakkuk began to deliver God's message to Judah. The two southern tribes, Judah and Benjamin, had enjoyed much prosperity and ease. They had gotten so caught up in themselves that they had drifted far away from what God wanted them to do (2 Chronicles 36:1-4). Their kings and priests were wicked and selfish. They had turned to worshipping idols, ignoring the one true God. It was God who loved, protected and blessed them so richly. When mankind gets so smart and proud of what he can do for himself, he seems to always turn his back on God. The children of Israel were behaving like rebellious, spoiled children and it was time for God to punish them for their disobedience.

- Do you ever think you know more or are smarter than your parents? _____ Name the situation. _____
_____

The Edomites, Assyrians and Chaldeans (also called Babylonians) were the chief nations who afflicted the Jews. Three prophets were sent to pronounce these three wicked nations' destruction. Obadiah foretells the destruction of the Edomites (c. 845 B.C.), Nahum foretells the destruction of the Assyrians (c. 630 B.C.) and Habakkuk pronounces the destruction of the Chaldeans (c. 612-605 B.C.). Such a prophecy would be a great encouragement to Judah in this scary time of pending war.

A large portion of Habakkuk is devoted to conversation between God and the prophet himself. This book is different from other books of prophecy. Instead of a message by Jehovah to the people, the prophet takes the complaint of the people to Jehovah. Habakkuk addresses God with a series of questions such as, "Why does wickedness seem to triumph and the righteous suffer?" (1:2-4). Explain this verse in your own words. _____
_____

God does not settle His account as man does: God's people are to wait for Him. They are assured that God will not fail them (2:2-4).

The story begins with Habakkuk crying to God because of Judah's wickedness and disregard for the law. Habakkuk asks God, "How long can this continue?" God replies that He is sending the Chaldeans to bring His judgment upon Judah. This news sent the prophet to his knees. While Habakkuk is presenting the complaints of the people to God, the Chaldean army has already begun its ruthless, destructive path toward Judah. Habakkuk asks how God could punish Judah by using a nation more wicked than itself. Wherever evil is found, its own destruction will follow. God points out that the righteous man will live by faith. As Habakkuk and the few righteous people who still lived in Judah discover, they must wait for God. God tells Habakkuk that Judah's sins have condemned her to destruction. The tool or instrument by which that destruction will come, whether righteous or wicked, does not matter. If the oppressors are evil, like the Chaldeans, then they too will face their own destruction. Only in righteousness is there life; sin always brings death.

When Habakkuk understands that the fall of lawless Judah was really going to happen, he decides to wait on God's judgment that would soon come through the terrible and cruel attack of the Chaldean army. When he finally understands God's plan to deliver justice to His people, he records one of the most beautiful expressions of faith found in the Bible. Read Chapter 3:19. " The LORD God is my _____; He will make my _____ like deer's feet, and He will make me walk on my _____ _____."

God's message is clear and Habakkuk announces it to the world—God permits and uses wicked nations to accomplish His divine purpose but in the end the wicked must be punished. Habakkuk concludes by praising God's wisdom even though he does not fully understand God's way.

Things to think about

- God brings judgment upon the wicked. God used Babylon against wicked Judah, but in time, Babylon would also be destroyed because of its own wickedness. God tolerated wickedness for a short time, but wicked Babylon must reap its reward for its own sins.

- Faithfulness is an outward display for staying true to God. If the righteous will be patient, they will survive tyranny (oppression). Evil is self-destructive.

- God is just and will administer discipline. Because of their wickedness and stubborn rebellion, the entire nation of Judah was punished. Times of suffering and punishment may bring us to godly sorrow. Godly sorrow may bring us to true repentance (2 Cor. 7:10). An absolute trust in God will keep you from doubting and having fears (Prov. 3:5-6). This is a lesson for all men not just for the people of Judah during Habakkuk's time. Have you ever done something and then felt sorry for doing it? _____.

Questions

1. What does the name Habakkuk mean? _____

2. In your own words, what would you say is the message of the book? ____

3. What has just happened to Israel? _____

4. Who is the king over Judah at the time Habakkuk is prophesing? _____ What are some of his evil deeds? _____
   _____
   _____

5. What is so confusing to Habakkuk about the method that God chooses to judge Judah? _____
   _____
   _____

6. What is meant in Habakkuk 2:20, that "all the earth should *keep silent* before the Lord in His Holy Temple?" _____
   _____
   _____
   _____

7. How do you develop trust in God? _____
   _____
   _____

Mapping the Minor Prophets

Fill in the blanks with the letter or number that corresponds to the map locations listed below.

Bodies of Water

____ Persian Gulf
____ Sea of Galilee
____ Dead Sea
____ Jordan River
____ Tigris River
____ Euphrates River
____ Mediterranean Sea

Nations

____ Judah
____ Babylonian Empire

Cities

____ Babylon
____ Jerusalem

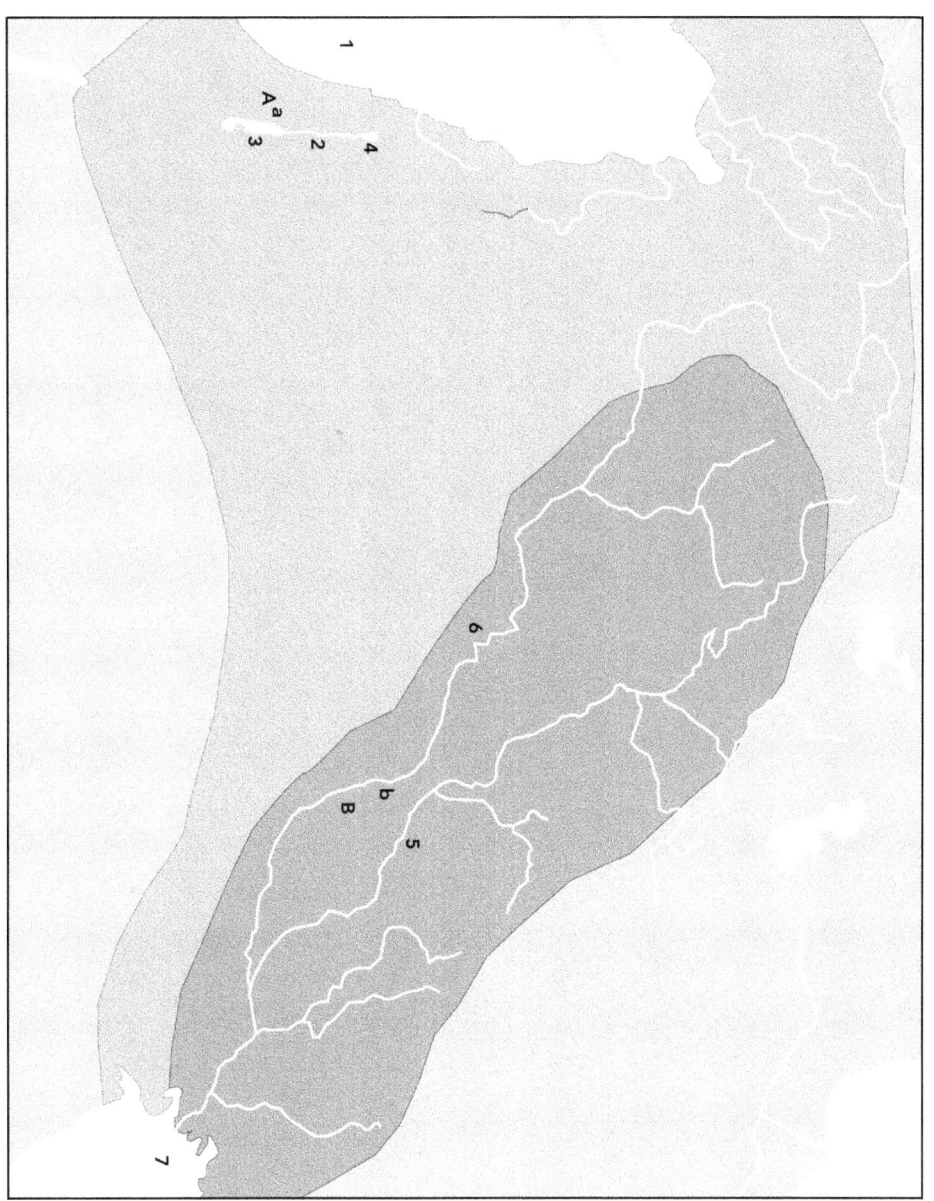

Lesson 10

ZEPHANIAH
pronounced: zeh-fuh-NAI-uh

Reading Assignment
Zephaniah

Who was Zephaniah?

KEY FACTS TO REMEMBER	
Where was Zephaniah from	Jerusalem
To whom did he prophesy	Judah
Key Verses	Zephaniah 3:8
Memory Key	Approaching doom at "the great Day of the Lord."

Zephaniah is the son of Cushi, the great-great grandson of king Hezekiah. It is believed that he is the only prophet of royal descent. His name means Jehovah hides, Jehovah has hidden or treasured. "This place" suggests that Jerusalem was his home (Zeph. 1:4).

When was it written?

He prophesied during the days of King Josiah from 630-625 B.C. and was very familiar with the conditions of the city of Jerusalem (1:4). He prophesied to Judah about 40 years before the nation fell captive to Babylon.

Zephaniah prophesied during the same time period as Habakkuk, Nahum, and the major prophet, Jeremiah. Whether any of these prophets of God knew or worked with each other is unknown, the Scriptures simply do not reveal that information.

What was the Message?

Manasseh was one of the more wicked kings in Judah's history (2 Kgs 21:1-9, 16; 2 Chron. 33:1-9). He was responsible for the murders of a great number of people in Judah. After Judah enjoyed the reign of good king Hezekiah, his wicked son Manasseh came to the throne of Judah. After King Amon's death, his young son Josiah came to the throne at the age of eight. He was the last good king to rule over Judah.

- Have you seen good kids come from bad parents and bad kids come from good parents? _____.

At the young age of 20, Josiah made great efforts to reform Judah. Pagan altars and idol images were destroyed and the bones of the wicked priests, who had offered sacrifices on the altars of false gods, were gathered and burned. In the cleansing of the temple, a copy of the book of the Law was found. Josiah ordered it to be read to all the people. After the Temple was cleansed the Passover was again observed. The Passover had not been kept for many years (2Kgs 22-23; 2 Chron 34-35). It was during this time that God sent his prophet Zephaniah to warn the people to remove all the sin they had became comfortable with under Manasseh's reign and turn back to God.

- Do you think you can escape from sin or the consequences of sin? _____

- Name a sin you have committed and the consequence you received.
_____
_____

Zephaniah warned Judah that God's judgment was coming upon every sinner. The 'Great Day of the Lord' was very near (1:14)! [1]Zephaniah was clear with his warning that all people who sin would suffer the consequences of their sin—no one would be able to run from God's judgment. To help the people understand God's judgments, they were to look to the nations around them to see how God punished those nations that refused to repent. God can certainly root up and destroy any nation on earth. They cannot hide themselves from His righteous judgments.

Zephaniah told Judah that their judgment was near because of their rebellion to God. After their judgment, God would gather those who had remained faithful to Him. Those faithful few are often referred to as the faithful remnant. Their enemies had been cast out and they did not need to fear evil any more. Zephaniah described the future hope and comfort in the coming of Christ. Those who wait on the Lord will see how the Lord will accomplish His purposes and bring down all kingdoms of men (3:8).

Things to think about:

- It is troublesome to think God sent four of His prophets to warn his people of the wrath and judgment He was going to bring upon them if they continued in their wicked ways and still they refused to hear the

---

1 The term, Day of the Lord always indicates a judgment of some type to take place. It does not refer only to the final Judgment Day when the Lord returns to earth, His final judgment, the end of time.

warnings and return to God. Why do we sometime refuse to listen to God's warnings today? _____

Today, we have the Bible that records the prophets' warnings as well as physical evidence of God's righteous judgment, both from historical and archeological records. When we see nations falling into the same sinful patterns as the ancient cultures, do we ever stop to consider that the great and unchanging God does not hesitate to punish the wicked nations of our time in the same manner He did during the prophets' times? _____

- What does it take to get our attention as a person or as a nation? Must God send droughts, famine, floods or conquering nations to get our attention? God is long suffering. He wants all men to love, obey and spend an eternity with Him after this life is over. How long before God says, "Enough!" and brings judgment upon those that refuse all the warnings? We are so fortunate today that we can read about the warnings God sent through his faithful prophets. We can read about the stubborn hearts and punishments God allowed to come to those who refused to submit to His will. What makes a stubborn heart? _____ _____ We can read about those who were faithful to God and the protection He gave them when times were difficult.

- Men should seek the Lord. He is not far from us unless we put up walls of sin or indifference. When we humble our own will and submit to God's will, we know the joy of finding the Lord. Zephaniah 3:8 encourages us to _____ for the Lord.

Questions

1. Zephaniah is of royal decent through which king of Judah? _____
_____

2. Zephaniah was most likely from what city? _____

3. To whom is he prophesying? _____
_____

4. Who are some other minor prophets delivering God's messages at the same time? _____
_____

5. Who is a major prophet that would have prophesied at this time? _____
_____

6. What is Zephaniah's message to the people of Judah? _____
_____
_____

7. What nation from the North was threatening Judah at this time? _____
_____

8. After seeing God's judgments on the nations surrounding them, how does Zephaniah hope Judah would respond? _____
_____
_____

9. As we read Zephaniah's message, can we apply it to ourselves today? What is your response to it? _____
_____

Mapping the Minor Prophets

Fill in the blanks with the letter or number that corresponds to the map locations listed below.

Bodies of Water

____ Dead Sea
____ Jordan River
____ Mediterranean Sea
____ Persian Gulf
____ Sea of Galilee

Nations

____ Babylonian Empire
____ Judah

Cities

____ Jerusalem
____ Babylon

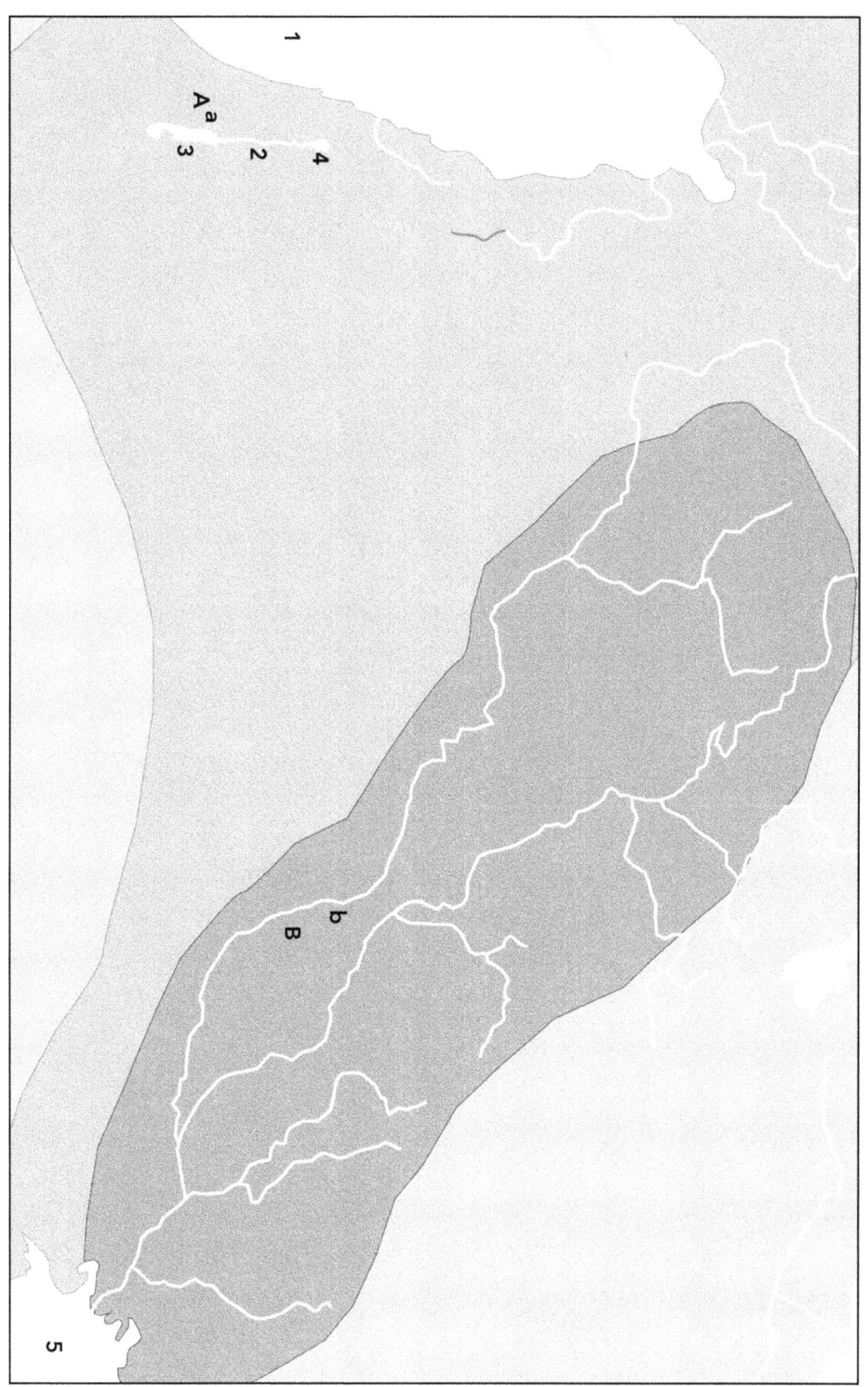

Lesson 11

HAGGAI
pronounced: HAG-ay-ai

Reading Assignment
Haggai

Who was Haggai?

Haggai, along with Zechariah and Malachi, are three prophets belonging to the period after the return from Babylonian captivity. They are referred to as post-

KEY FACTS TO REMEMBER

Where was Haggai from	Judah (after the return from Babylonian captivity)
To whom did he prophesy	Jews returning home
Key Verses	Haggai 1:7-8
Memory Key	Stop being selfish and rebuild the Lord's house, put God first.

exilic prophets. All we are told about Haggai is simply that he was a prophet. It is assumed that he was probably one of the exiles that could remember the beauty and grandeur of Solomon's Temple before its destruction. If this were a true assumption, then Haggai would have been at least 75 years of age.

The literal meaning of the name Haggai is festival, festive or the joyous one. He appeals frequently to Jehovah as the source of his word. Haggai is one of the shortest books of the Bible and was once referred to as 'a momentous little fragment.'

When was it written?

The book of Ezra confirms that Haggai was among the first remnant of Jews to return from Babylonian captivity in 536 B.C. Haggai dates his work as "in the second year of Darius the king" which would have occurred in the summer of 520 B.C. (1:1). Haggai records a total of four messages from God, which occurred over the course of four months (1:1; 2:1; 2:10; 2:20).

In 586 B.C. the Babylonians destroyed Jerusalem and the Temple. The conquering Babylonians then fell to the Persians in 539 B.C. One year later,

King Cyrus issued a decree that the various exiles could return to their own lands and rebuild their Temple (2 Chron. 36:22, 23; Ezra 1).

- Why do you think Cyrus allowed the Jews to return? _____
_____
_____

Approximately 50,000 exiles returned from Babylon under the leadership of Zerubbabel in 536 B.C. It is interesting to note that some 150 years earlier, Isaiah (one of the major prophets) had prophesied that Jehovah would raise up Cyrus who would allow a remnant to return to Jerusalem (Isa 44:24-45:7). Upon their return to Jerusalem, the Jews restored the altar of sacrifices to Jehovah and laid the foundation of the Temple. It was at this point that the work on the Temple ceased.

- Why did the temple work halt? _____
_____
_____

In the second year of Darius I, (also known as Darius Hystaspes who reigned from 522-486 B.C. and not to be confused with Darius the Mede, who ruled earlier) Haggai and Zechariah were called to arouse the Jews to complete the work on the Temple that had been started 16 years earlier (Ezra 4:1-24). In 520 B.C. the Temple project resumed and was finished in 515 B.C. (Ezra 6:14-15).

What was the Message?

Ezra 5:1 and 6:14 announce the simple and straightforward message, "Build the temple!"

It was at this point that God sent His prophets, Haggai and Zechariah to stir the people out of their spiritual indifference. Spiritual indifference is when one neither approves nor denies the power of God and His Word. We must have conviction in that what we believe is truth.

- What things help convict you of your faith? _____
_____
_____

Almost as quickly as the work to rebuild the Temple started, it stopped. The people were more concerned about working on their own homes and life styles than completing the *house of the Lord.* The prophet warned, "*Now therefore, thus says the LORD of hosts: Consider your ways! You have sown much, and bring in little; You eat, but do not have enough; You drink, but you are not filled with drink; You clothe yourselves, but no one is warm; And he who earns wages, Earns wages to put into a bag with holes. Thus says the LORD of hosts: Consider your ways! Go up to the mountains and bring wood and build the temple, that I may take pleasure in it and be glorified, says the LORD. You looked for much, but indeed it came to little; and when you brought it home, I blew it away. Why? says the LORD of hosts. Because of My house that is in ruins, while every one of you runs to his own house,"* (Hag. 1:5-9).

- Do you ever get you priorities wrong? _____
- What are some things people put before God? _____
  _____
  _____

Their priorities were all wrong, thus they had not received the fullness of God's blessings because they had placed their wants before God. Within 3 weeks after Haggai delivered his message from God, the people responded and resumed their work on the Temple.

In 515 B.C. the Temple was completed (Ezra 6:15). Speaking through Haggai, God told the exiles, who saw and remembered the glory of the former Temple, to be strong for He was with them just like He was when they came out of Egypt. "The glory of this present house will be greater than the glory of the former house," says the Lord Almighty. The Temple they were now looking at did not even remotely compare with the beauty or grandeur of the Temple Solomon built for God so many years earlier. Those elderly exiles that had seen the former Temple did remember and they cried. It is interesting to think that this lesser, more modest Temple, will be the one that our Lord and Savior, Jesus Christ would someday walk within; that was something Solomon's Temple could never claim.

- Why would the glory of the present temple be greater than the former one? _____
  _____

God renewed the promise of salvation with the Messianic hope preserved through Zerubbabel (2:23). This fact is indeed fulfilled in that Zerubbabel was in the direct lineage of Jesus (Matt 1:12; Lk 3:27). Haggai states "Zerubbabel would be as a signet" (seal of authority).

Things to think about

- Priorities matter. We will never find happiness or real contentment in this life if we allow anything or anyone to come before God (Hag 2:15-19; Matt 6:33, Lk 14:16-24; 1 Tim 6:6-10, 17-19). What can you do to keep God first in your life? _____
  _____
  _____

- When we put our trust in material possessions we will never be rich toward God. Rather we will soon learn just how 'spiritually poor' we really are (Matt 6:19; 10:37; 1 Tim 6:10).

Questions:

1. What does 'post-exile' mean? _____
_____

2. What king allowed the Jews to return to Jerusalem and what did he want them to do? _____
_____

3. Who is Zerubbabel and who is his famous descendant? _____
_____
_____

4. What does it mean to be spiritually indifferent? _____
_____
_____

5. What are the busy people doing and what are they suppose to be doing?
_____
_____
_____

6. What are some of the "clues" that show their activities are not pleasing to God? _____
_____
_____

7. What is Haggai's message? _____
_____
_____
_____

Haggai ■ 77

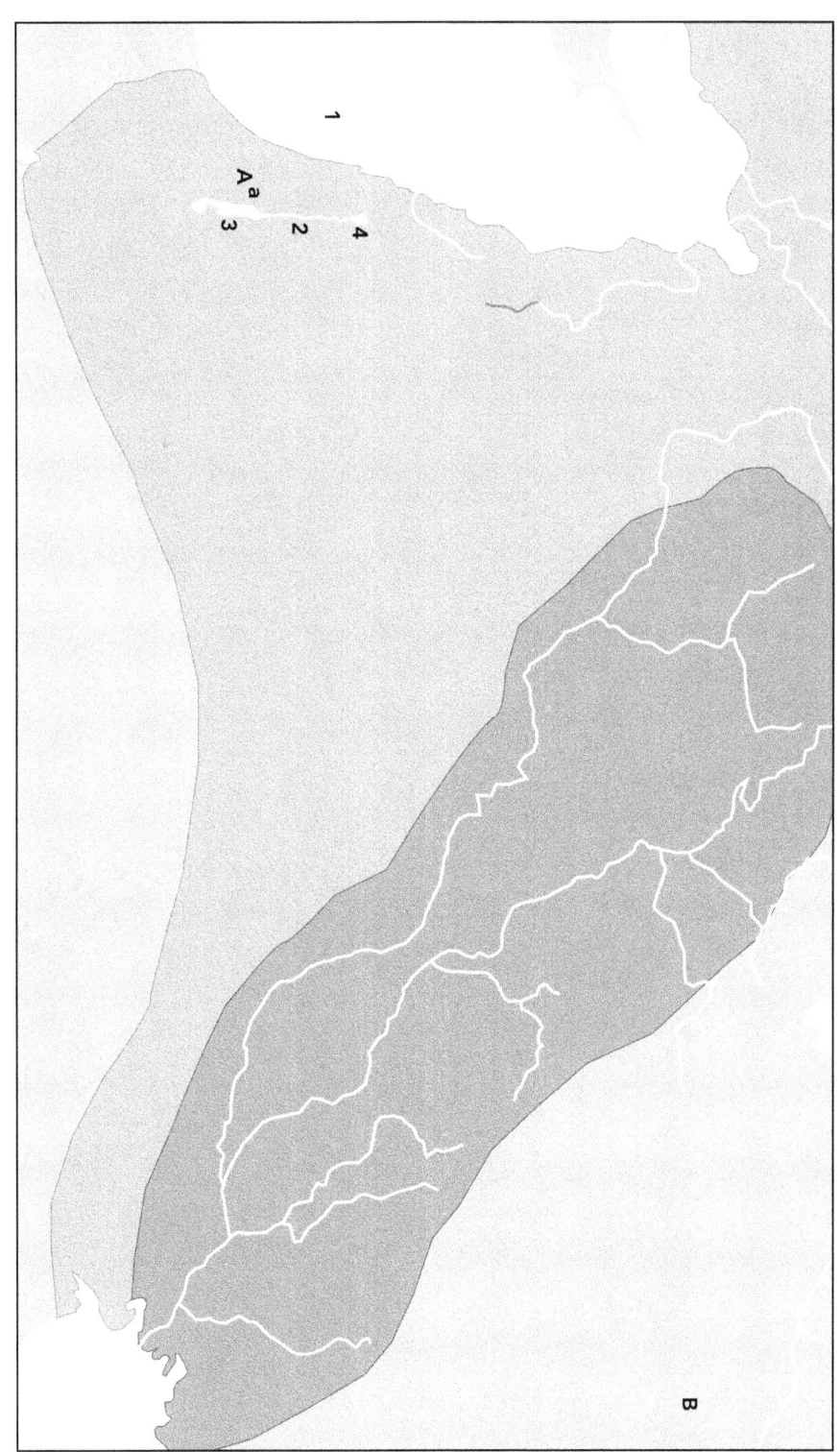

Mapping the Minor Prophets

Fill in the blanks with the letter or number that corresponds to the map locations listed below.

Bodies of Water

____ Jordan River
____ Mediterranean Sea
____ Sea of Galilee
____ Dead Sea

Nations

____ Returning Exiles of Judah
____ Persian Empire

Cities

____ Jerusalem

Lesson 12

ZECHARIAH
pronounced: zeh-kuh-RAI-uh

Reading Assignment
Zechariah

Who was Zechariah?

Zechariah means, whom Jehovah remembers. This was a popular name among Hebrew families. Zechariah is the son of Berechiah, the grandson of Iddo,

KEY FACTS TO REMEMBER

Where was Zechariah from	Born in Babylonian captivity
To whom did he prophesy	The Jews who had returned to Jerusalem
Key Verses	Zehariah 6:13
Memory Key	Return to the Lord and rebuild the temple

and is of priestly descent (1:1). It is Zechariah's grandfather, Iddo, who was listed among the group of priests being led by Zerubbabel in the return from Babylonian captivity to Jerusalem in 536 B.C. (Neh 12:4, 16). Zechariah is also a co-worker with the prophet Haggai (Ezra 5:1; 6:14).

When was it written?

Part of the book of Zechariah was written during the second year of King Darius of Persia, 520 B.C. (1:1, 7). This is also the same time that the entire book of Haggai was written. Zechariah 7:1 tells us that another part of the book was written in the fourth year of King Darius, 518 B.C. We learn in Ezra 6:14 that both Zechariah and Haggai continued to prophesy until the Temple was completely rebuilt.

Both Zechariah and Haggai were most likely born while in Babylonian captivity and returned to Jerusalem together. Zechariah is the longest book of the Minor Prophets and is frequently quoted in the New Testament—it is also the most difficult to understand. His style of prophecy is called Apocalyptic—that means an unveiling, revealing or uncovering. This style of writing is also described as figurative because of the use of visions, numbers and characters to point to future events. Much of Zechariah's writings tell of future Messianic events—the coming of the Christ.

What was the Message?

The main focus of this book is to encourage the people, who had returned from Babylonian captivity, to fully return their lives to the Lord. The people started the work to rebuild the Temple by restoring the altar of sacrifices and laying the foundation of the Temple, but then the work stopped! For 16 years no work was done on the Temple. The people were content to take care of their own wants and comforts before doing God's work. It was Haggai and Zechariah's job to get the Jewish people back to work and complete the Temple. In 520 B. C., the people started back to work on the Temple.

- What are some ways we do what we want instead of doing what the Lord wants? Is this selfish behavior? _____
  _____
  _____
  _____

Zechariah reminded the people that the prophets before them had been sent to warn their fathers to repent, but they refused. Because of their stubbornness, God brought judgment on those who refused to listen and obey. Two months after Haggai's last recorded prophecy, Zechariah received the first of eight night visions:

1. The vision of the Horsemen (1:7-11)
   Purpose—to assure them that the Temple of God would be rebuilt.

2. The vision of the Horns and Craftsmen (1:18-21)
   Purpose—God will cast down the enemy powers for their evil ways and idolatries.
   The four horns represented the four world powers that scattered Israel and Judah. The four craftsmen were coming to cast out the horns.

3. The vision of the Measuring Line (2:1-5)
   Purpose—Jerusalem would be restored but God's bigger plan and purpose was to build a spiritual Jerusalem that would be unlimited in size.

4. The vision of the High Priest (3:1-5)
   Purpose—to make known the cleansing of the priesthood to purify them in order to offer sacrifices for the people and lead them back to God.

The Angel of the Lord then told the high priest, Joshua, that if he would continue to be faithful, God would do something even greater for His people; He would send the "Branch" (3:8). This was Messianic, referencing the coming of Christ.

> 5. The vision of the Lampstand and Olive Trees (4:1-14)
> Purpose—a message to Zerubbabel that God would help him finish his work to rebuild the Temple. The two olive trees represent Zerubbabel, the government leader, and Joshua, the high priest, who was the religious leader. Matthew 1:12 also lists Zerubbabel in the lineage of Christ. Jesus is both King and High Priest, a position held by only one other mentioned in the Bible, Melchizedek in Genesis 14:18 and Hebrews 7:1-3; 17. The Lampstand represented God's Spirit.
>
> 6. The vision of the Flying Scroll (5:1-4)
> Purpose—to show that God's curse would be upon the dishonest
>
> 7. The vision of the Woman in a Basket (5:5-11)
> Purpose—to show that when the Temple was rebuilt, the land would be free from wickedness. The woman in the basket represents wickedness and was carried away.
>
> 8. The vision of the Four Chariots (6:1-8)
> Purpose—God is in control; the earth is at peace under God's protection.

Zechariah is filled with many Messianic prophecies speaking of the coming of Christ and His Kingdom. Chapter 6:11-13 tells of the crowning of Joshua, the high priest. This is figurative. Joshua was not qualified to be a king since he was not from the tribe of Judah. However, he was "crowned" to symbolize the coronation of Jesus, also referred to as the *Branch* and *My Servant the Branch*. The *Branch* is Jesus Christ coming from the *Tree* of David. He would be raised from the dead to build His spiritual temple, the church. He would ascend to Heaven to rule on His throne and be the great High Priest.

- List the lineage (family tree) of Jesus starting with Abraham (Matt. 1).
  _____
  _____
  _____
  _____
  _____

Zechariah pleaded for the people to remember the results of the hardening of their hearts as they refused to obey God. He then announced God's judgments against the wicked nations. As always, God is faithful to His word and fulfills His promises, in His time. History confirms the destruction of each one of these nations.

In chapter 9:7-8, we once again see that God fights for and protects all those who believe in Him. Living under the Messiah's care, God's children are gathered from among all the nations of the earth and given spiritual blessings and strength. While there is a happy restoration of those faithful to God, there seems to always be those among God's people who are rebellious and unfaithful. True to His word, God deals with those who are stubborn, rebellious and unfaithful. He will deliver a divine judgment. "*It is a fearful thing to fall into the hands of the living God*" (Heb. 10:31).

- What are some ways we can be stubborn and rebellious? _____
  _____
  _____

- Why is it a fearful thing to fall into God's hands? _____
  _____
  _____

While these prophecies would be partly fulfilled in the return from the captivity, they are fully realized in the Messianic reign when spiritual Israel is united with Christ in battle against the forces of spiritual darkness (Eph 6:10-12).

Things to think about

- Just as the prophet Zechariah and others offered comfort to God's people, we today can also take comfort in knowing that God's plan is still in place. All the enemies of God and His people will be defeated. God wins!

- What is God's plan? _____
  _____
  _____

- How will the enemies of God be defeated? _____
  _____
  _____

- God was very specific about what sacrifices He would accept from His people. The sacrifice had to be perfect, not sick, blind or lame. Yet, the priest would offer damaged, less than perfect offerings to God. Not only was such sacrifice unacceptable to God, it was an insult to Him. He wants our best not our "leftovers." What do you offer the Lord? Do you put Him first in all that you do or do you try to fit Him in behind your many responsibilities and activities? God wants to be first in our hearts. He will not accept second place.

- Name ways you put God first. _____
  _____
  _____

- Name things that you have put before worship and God. _____
  _____
  _____
  _____

Questions

1. What does the name Zechariah mean? _____
   _____

2. Who is the other prophet working during the same time as Zechariah? __
   _____

3. To whom was he sent to prophesy? _____
   _____

4. What is his message? _____
   _____
   _____

5. What are some things that make this book different from the other Minor Prophets? _____
   _____
   _____

6. Define the word Apocalyptic. _____
   _____
   _____

7. List the 8 visions Zechariah saw. _____
   _____
   _____
   _____
   _____
   _____

8. What does the word 'Messianic' mean? _____
   _____

9. What do you do to make God a priority in your day? _____
   _____
   _____

Mapping the Minor Prophets

Fill in the blanks with the letter or number that corresponds to the map locations listed below.

Bodies of Water

____ Sea of Galilee
____ Mediterranean Sea
____ Dead Sea
____ Jordan River

Nations

____ Returning Exiles of Judah
____ Persian Empire

Cities

____ Jerusalem

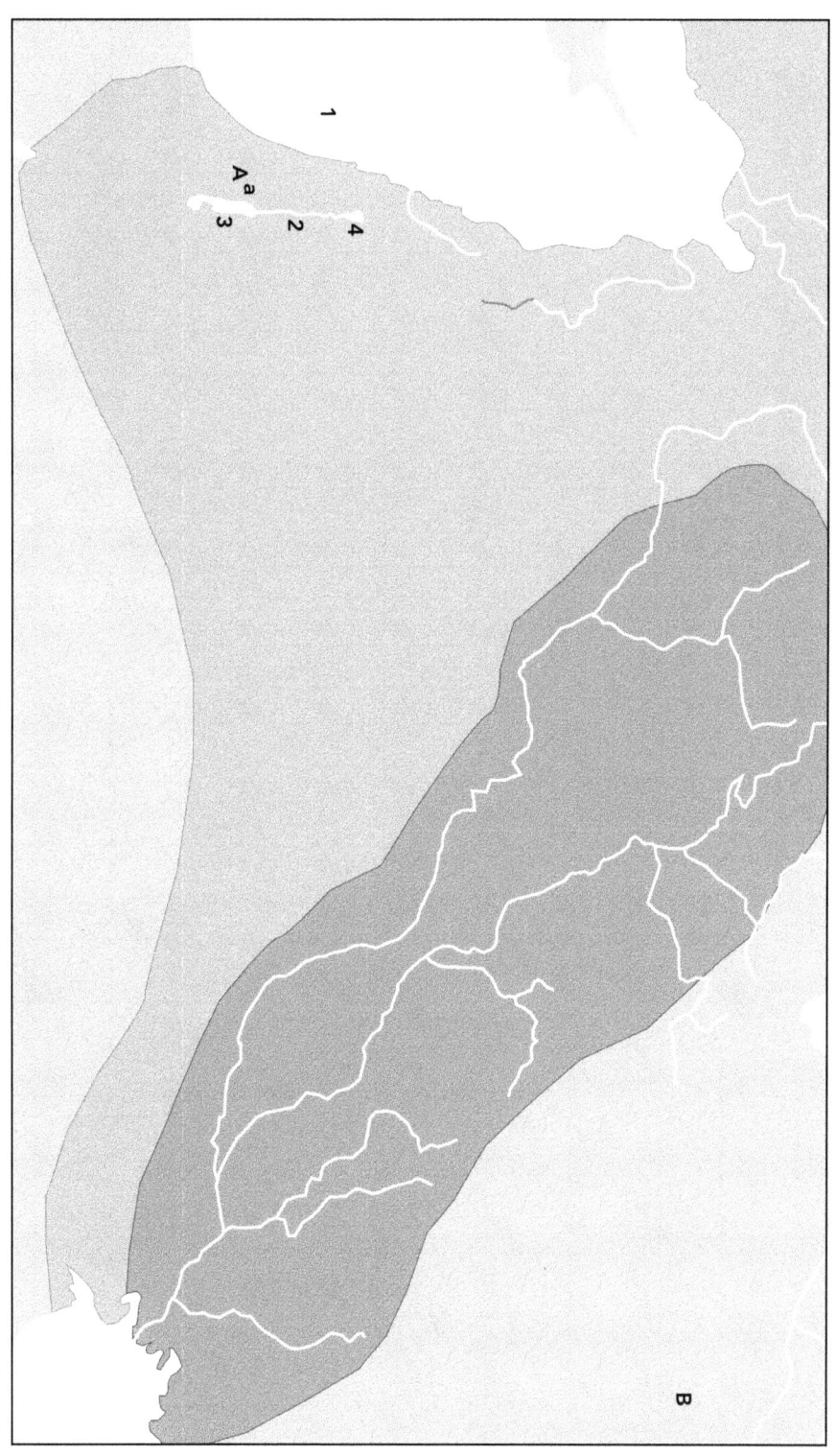

MALACHI
pronounced: MAL-uh-kai

Reading Assignment
Malachi

Who was Malachi?

Malachi is the last prophet mentioned in the Old Testament. His name simply means my messenger. Nothing more is known about this prophet other than the book that bears his name. His book is the last message from God before the coming of the Messiah. There is a period of 400 years that God does not send prophets to talk to His people. This is called the 'between the Testament' period and it covers a span of time from the last word of Malachi to the birth announcement of John the Baptist.

KEY FACTS TO REMEMBER

Where was Malachi from	A Jewish exile from Babylon
To whom did he prophesy	Returned exiles in Jerusalem
Key Verses	Malachi 4:5
Memory Key	Last Old Testament prophet to speak before 400 years of silence; announcment of John the Baptist

When was it written?

Malachi prophesied during the reign of Artaxerxes I, 465-423 B.C. This was during the time Nehemiah led the last group of exiles out of Babylon and back to Jerusalem in 445 B.C. It could be said that the prophet Malachi was to Nehemiah what Haggai and Zechariah had been to Zerubbabel.

The social conditions that Malachi dealt with in his book compare to those of the Persian period described by Nehemiah. This was a time when serious abuses had crept into Jewish life:

- The priests had become careless and sloppy.
- Flawed and unacceptable sacrifices were allowed to be offered upon the temple altar.

- The people were not tithing (offering a tenth of their profits to God).
- Divorce had become a common practice.
- The Jews were putting away their wives and marrying foreign women.

For a full description of the horrible conditions in Judea at this time, read Ezra 7-10 and the book of Nehemiah.

- List five conditions of Judah and the verse describing the conditon.
  1. _____
  2. _____
  3. _____
  4. _____
  5. _____

What was the Message?

The style of the book is a series of accusations (or charges) followed by questions and then another accusation to prove the point. (Example: You stole the cookie. Were you in the kitchen? Do you like cookies? etc.) It is called 'didactic-dialectic'. It reads like a lecture followed with debate. This style makes Malachi the most argumentative of all the prophets of the Old Testament.

Malachi assured Israel of God's unchanging love for them and their need to return their love to Him in faithfulness. He showed this love in a contrast made between Israel and Edom (Jacob and Esau). Malachi then began to list the sinful acts that Israel continued to offer to God. He started with the offerings the priests presented to God. They offered the spoiled, damaged offerings and then acted like they didn't know why God was not happy with their offerings. The Lord spoke through Malachi asking the people to offer up the stolen, ruined and/or damaged offerings to their governor and see if he would be happy with their gifts.

Malachi told the people there would be a time when God's name would be great not only among the Jewish nation but among all nations. This was a Messianic prophecy looking to the time when God would welcome the Gentile nations into His family if they would believe, turn away from sin and obey Him.

The priests acted as if they were tired of following God's rules—it was a big burden to them. The lazy priests were warned that if they did not give glory to God and offer approved sacrifices to Him, then a curse would come upon them. God would not tolerate their sloppy, halfhearted service.

- Do you ever "tire" of following God's rules? _____

- List some things God expects you to do that you do not understand and find hard to follow. _____
_____
_____
_____
_____

Because the priests failed in their teaching of God's way, the people committed sin by divorcing their Jewish wives and marrying foreign wives. These foreign women brought their idol gods with them and caused Israel to sin against God. God says, He "hates divorce" because of the violence and hurt that it brings to a home and everyone in it.

- Is it our responsibility to know ALL of God's Word (Psa. 139:17)? _____
_____

- What are some dangers if we don't? _____
_____
_____

The people wickedly accused God of favoring evildoers over them. God answered them by saying "*I send My messenger and he will prepare the way before Me*" (3:1). This is fulfilled when John the Baptist comes some 400 years later to announce the coming of the Messiah, Jesus the Christ. When the Messiah comes He will apply the judgment of God—He will separate those who are faithful from the disobedient.

God says, "*I am the Lord, I do not change*" (3:6). He does not judge the wicked one day and then delight in their wickedness the next. He is the same and requires obedience to His laws from all men for all time. The people ask, "But what have we done wrong?" Malachi answers with the question, "Will a man rob God?" Yes, they had robbed God. They had not given to the Lord as they should have (3:8). The whole nation was guilty of robbing God by neglecting to return a tenth of their profits back to God. God despised their halfhearted service.

There are always those who are wanting to please and obey God. Malachi tells us that those precious few who fear and obey God have their names written in a book of remembrances. Even if they are few in number, what a comfort to know that God knows the names and deeds of His faithful.

The final word of the Old Testament from the book of Malachi is an encouragement to all men to turn to God and repent, or expect severe divine judgment. "*The day of the Lord is coming like a burning oven to consume the wicked*" (4:1). They are to keep the Law of Moses and watch and wait. Four hundred years later, the promised messenger, John the Baptist, came preparing the way for the Messiah, the Lamb of God, the Christ who would take away the sins of the world.

Things to think about

- All Christians today are priests before God. They are to present themselves "as a living sacrifice, holy and acceptable to God." To do this we must carefully listen to the warnings of God. We need to be faithful in knowing the truth, obeying it, and teaching it to others. Laziness and carelessness causes our Spiritual sacrifices to be unacceptable to God. (Rom 12:1; Heb 13:15).

- The Law of Moses was difficult to keep. Jesus was the only one to keep it perfectly—all other Israelites failed when trying to keep it. The priests offered an animal sacrifice on the altar in the morning and again in the evening. They did this every day from the time God gave Moses the Law until the church was established in A.D. 33. Can you imagine how many helpless animals were killed, how many rivers of blood flowed because stubborn people refused to obey God? On the Day of Atonement, the High Priest entered the Holy of Holies and God would forgive the guilt of sin for one year. Only a perfect sacrifice could totally remove sin; animal sacrifice could not do that. Jesus was that perfect sacrifice. He was totally without sin in His life. Jesus, the Lamb of God, was the only sacrifice that could completely erase sin. Jesus, God's only Son, allowed himself to be offered as a sacrifice for the sins of all mankind for all time (Heb 10: 1-18).

Questions

1. Who is Malachi? _____

2. To whom did God send Malachi to prophesy? _____

3. What is the religious condition at the time? _____
_____

4. What do the foreign wives bring with them that cause their Jewish husbands to sin? _____
_____

5. How does God feel about divorce? _____
_____

6. Why does Malachi say the people robbed God? _____
_____
_____
_____

7. In what way can we rob God today? _____
_____
_____
_____

8. Malachi was the last of God's Old Testament prophets sent to warn the people to repent. How many years before God speaks to the people again? _____

9. What event in the New Testament occurrs when God again reveals Himself to man? _____
_____
_____

10. How are we like priests today? _____
_____
_____
_____

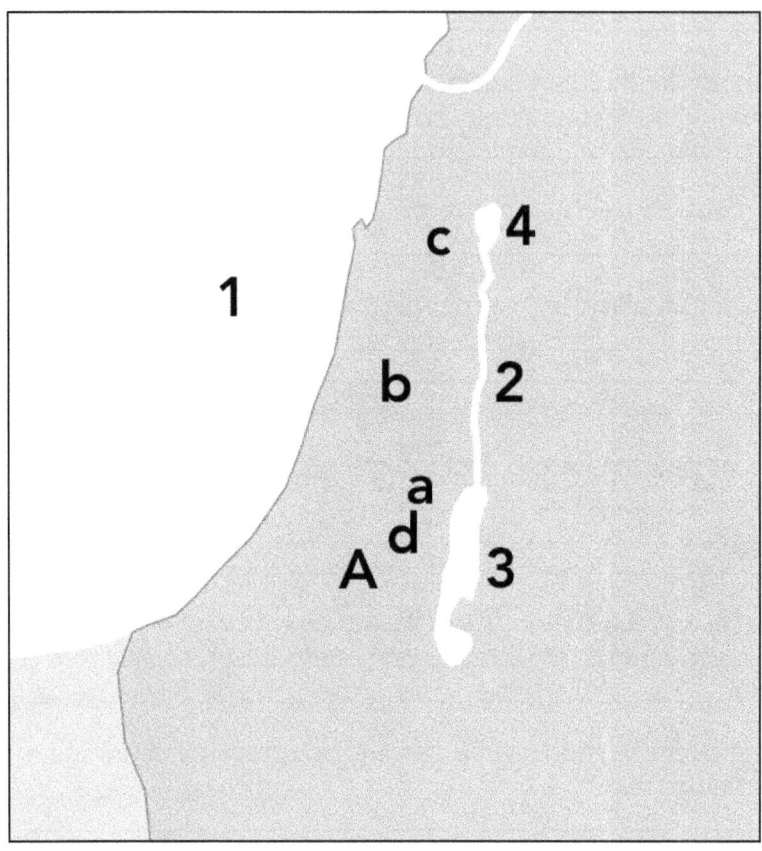

Mapping the Minor Prophets

Fill in the blanks with the letter or number that corresponds to the map locations listed below.

Bodies of Water

____ Mediterranean Sea
____ Jordan River
____ Dead Sea
____ Sea of Galilee

Cities

____ Galilee
____ Bethlehem
____ Jerusalem
____ Samaria

Nations

____ Returning Exiles of Judah